Keeping Your Balance

Keeping Your Balance

Marilee Horton
Walter Byrd, M.D.

WORD BOOKS
PUBLISHER
WACO, TEXAS

A DIVISION OF
WORD, INCORPORATED

Our gratitude to Karen Schon for her sweet spirit
during the many late hours of typing, changes,
and retyping.

KEEPING YOUR BALANCE: A WOMAN'S GUIDE TO PHYSICAL, EMO-
TIONAL, AND SPIRITUAL WELL-BEING
Copyright © 1984 by Marilee Horton and Walter Byrd, M.D.

"The Stress of Adjusting to Change" scale on p. 96–97 reprinted by permission
from *Psychosomatics*, 19: 747, 1978.

Unless otherwise marked, all Scripture quotations are from The Authorized King
James Version. Scripture quotations marked NASB are from the New American
Standard Bible, © The Lockman Foundation 1960, 1962, 1963, 1971, 1972,
1973, 1975, 1977; AMPLIFIED are from the *Amplified New Testament*, © The
Lockman Foundation 1954, 1958. Used by permission; RSV are from the Revised
Standard Version of the Bible, copyright 1946, 1952, © 1971, 1973 by the
National Council of the Churches of Christ in the U.S.A., and are used by
permission.

Library of Congress Cataloging in Publication Data:

Horton, Marilee.
  Keeping your balance.

    1. Women—Religious life.   2. Women—Psychology.
I. Byrd, Walter.   II. Title.
BV4527.H67   1984   248.8'43   84-10449
ISBN 0-8499-0399-8

Printed in the United States of America

I dedicate this book to Marvin, the one who has loved me during the search for balance, who has supported me at every stage, and has given my life fulfillment.

Marilee Horton

I dedicate this book to my wife, Karen, whose ever-present support made the writing of this book possible, and to my mother, Earline, whose nurturance made the becoming of a man possible.

Walter Byrd, M.D.

Contents

Foreword

This book provides an outstanding blend of spiritual wisdom, professional depth, personal wit, and realism. Marilee Horton and Walt Byrd are both well-experienced in their respective fields. Marilee brings her skills as a seasoned author, counselor, and widely traveled women's seminar speaker. Her personal struggles with some of the problems discussed in the book produce a level of practicality and empathy that is truly exceptional. Dr. Byrd's years of experience as a licensed pastor, physician, and psychiatrist provide the book with impressive spiritual and professional depth.

Together they extensively cover needs, problems, and answers to problems in all three dimensions of Christian womanhood— spirit, soul, and body.

I am delighted to see them writing together and I heartily recommend *Keeping Your Balance* to women everywhere who are interested in developing real balance and maturity in their lives.

Paul Meier, M.D.
Coauthor, *Happiness Is a Choice*

Introduction

To say I knew I was totally ill on that clear, fresh April morning when an expert intensive care staff unscrewed the life support system from my mouth is a vast understatement. Living had become so utterly painful that death softly beckoned me like a return to a dark, warm womb.

As I was rolled down a hall into a regular room I was cognizant of only three alternatives: Either I would find a way to rectify my thwarted suicide attempt by a method more sure than forty sleeping pills; I would drag through life, existing mainly for my family; or I would find out how to live a balanced, abundant life.

Coming out of the frayed, faded blue gown that didn't quite cover my sunken backside, I stood shocked at my own appearance. On wobbly, pencil-thin legs I was now slimmer than I had ever hoped or wanted to be, cheeks hollow and eyes like vacant, dark holes. My body had suffered the ravages of months of malnourishment as I gave in to depression and neglected eating until I became unable to eat. My body, emaciated, pasty, weak, was thirty-seven years old, and I wondered if it would make it to thirty-eight, even if my mind willed it.

My mind. That pointed to a more pervasive sickness, one that spread through my soul, making retreat into depression more comfortable and acceptable than emotional exploration. A sickness whose tentacles reached deeply into my soul and convinced me that I couldn't cope with harsh, ugly reality and bombarded me with threats that I would never be well enough to enjoy life—if life were even *meant* to be enjoyed.

As I slipped into the bottoms of a new pair of white pajamas, I remembered a verse I used in teaching children about God's cleansing using the white page of a "wordless book": "Wash me, and I shall be whiter than snow" (Ps. 51:7).

It gripped my heart and I knew I was sick spiritually as well as physically. I had failed God. I had disagreed with the Master Architect about His design and tried to destroy His work, though I didn't feel I was destroying a masterpiece—more like a weird, Andy Warhol piece of confused, muddled pop art. My life had become a surrealistic image of His intention. Could I regain fellowship with my heavenly Father? Did I want to bother? I knew many who had fallen by the wayside. Maybe I was just another casualty.

Reading a little note on yellow legal paper from my eleven-year-old daughter "Dear Mamma, please don't die" (which became the title of my first book), I had the first inkling of how totally ill I was—body, soul, and spirit.

That first book, about the suicide attempt and subsequent recovery, was written a bare two years after the events and looked as honestly as possible into as much as I could understand about causes and effects.

Nine years later—after sharing my story with thousands of women and counseling hundreds who say, "You must have crawled inside my head to write that book because I feel the very same way"—I knew I must share more:

What I have learned about me,
about you,
about my enemy,
and about living life to its fullest with the Living God.

It's about knowing and understanding. It's about being well and balanced, body, soul, and spirit.

This book encompasses the travel notes and recollections of the most incredible journey into one of God's most incredible designs—the human being.

Come, walk with me through the forest of these pages and praise

God with me if you have begun to find the secret of *balance*. Cry healing tears with me if you discover hidden emotional scars that *can* be healed. Rejoice with me as you too appropriate the abundant life that belongs to you as surely as the frame you were born with. Yes! Oh, yes! Life *is* meant to be enjoyed.

Where are you on your modern-day "pilgrim's progress"? Are you the proud owner of a jazzed-up and jogged-out, properly plucked and correctly coiffured body, only to find yourself parked too often at the "Slough of Despond" emotionally and spiritually?

Are you a spiritual giant in Sunday school and the prayer closet, but a basket case in the market where life in the fast lane hits the nitty-gritty?

Are you in control of your emotions, and is God in control of your spirit, but you present Christ in a generic, lackluster package instead of the neatest, most colorful, trim package possible, to attract others to Him?

What is balance? Why is it needed? Do you want it?

I am aware of arguments that we can't divide soul and spirit, but I'm willing to rest that with the following verses:

> For the word of God is quick, and powerful, and sharper than any two-edged sword, piercing even to the dividing asunder of soul and spirit, and of the joints and marrow, and is a discerner of the thoughts and intents of the heart (Heb. 4:12).

> And the very God of peace sanctify you wholly; and I pray God your whole spirit and soul and body be preserved blameless unto the coming of our Lord Jesus Christ (1 Thess. 5:23).

For the purpose of understanding ourselves well enough to get balanced, we will divide ourselves into three parts. *But* none of this will be done apart from the Word of God, seasoned with personal illustrations and humor.

PART I

The Body

Chapter 1
Introduction to the Body

Are You a Ming Vase or a Mason Jar?

I had a childish desire to press my nose against the protective glass case and stare at it as it sat in all its beauty on soft black velvet. I fought the urge and instead read the printed card beneath that rare and expensive Ming vase. It was hard to keep my eyes away from the fine oriental work of art. Dated between 1368–1644 during the Ming dynasty in China, the vase with gentle, flowing design was breathtaking. I remember the boys looking askance when I breathed aloud, "Perfect!"

Only one of our children at that age showed any interest in the arts so they whisked me on to more compelling sights at the space exhibit.

It is odd how that "perfect" vase viewed at a museum came to mind as I tried to understand a certain passage of Scripture as it pertains to women.

All scripture is given by inspiration of God, and is profitable for doctrine, for reproof, for correction, for instruction in righteousness:

That the man [woman] of God may be *perfect*, thoroughly furnished
unto all good works (2 Tim. 3:16–17, emphasis mine).

That word *perfect* grabbed me first, and then the phrase *thoroughly furnished*. During my months of recovery I somehow knew
instinctively that if I were to recover, the Word of God held the
key. But often I was stymied by descriptions like *perfect, thoroughly
furnished*. What did it mean? Did it mean we should just look
perfect or be perfectly functional?

I knew that on this earth I would never arrive at a sinlessly
perfect state but I also believed that given the right care and treatment I could be a functional work of art for the Lord.

After some digging I found that *perfect* has to do with keeping up
with the goal. The Greek word for thoroughly furnished, *exartizo*,
means "to accomplish; as if to render the days complete by what
was appointed for them."

Did it mean that by yielding to the Designer and Artist I could
be "perfect" or accomplish the goal He meant for me?

But, were beautiful Chinese vases from the Ming dynasty meant
just for sitting on velvet? No! Although most oriental objects are
now used strictly for ornamental purposes, they were designed
originally to be *utilitarian:* domestic vessels, sacrificial and ritu-
alistic vessels. Most of the handsome pieces exhibited in museums
were originally someone's kitchenware. Ming vases used to be
perfect; they were matchless in beauty, yet they accomplished the
purpose for which they were made, to be vessels. Now they are
only empty art objects to admire—useless.

When I ask for a show of hands at a seminar or retreat, nearly
everyone wants to be a Ming vase, but usually many hold up their
hands again to indicate they think they are really Mason jars. Do
women really want to be beautiful, but useless and empty vessels?
Which are you? Which would you rather be? Let's look at some
categories of women and see if you can identify yourself. You can
consciously choose to be either. We should keep in mind 2 Cor.
4:7, "But we have this treasure in earthen vessels, that the excel-
lency of the power may be of God, and not of us."

1. *Classic Ming vase.* Beautiful to behold but often empty because Christ has not been accepted as Lord. This often gifted woman offers only her talent, beauty, and human endeavor, as she adorns her community, home, and church. Perhaps unaware of the deep purposes Christ has for her, she busies herself by keeping her body in shape and decorative as she reads the latest "self-help" bestseller. Many churches are filled with these thoughtful, hard-working social reformers, and like the Ming vase, they may stand the test of time. But what about eternity? Good intentioned as some of these beautiful women are, they need to be careful not to fall under the critical judgment issued by the Lord to the spiritually lukewarm in Revelation 3:15–16, or to those who have only "done many wonderful works" in Matthew 7:22–23.

2. *Sealed Mason jar.* This woman, more than happy to be called a Christian, attends church every time the door is open. She loves Bible conferences and classes. She reads her Bible and prays. Her notebook gets fatter and fatter as she seeks the "deeper life." She doesn't believe in "pushing her beliefs" on others. There's the problem—she never takes the lid off to share the treasure she stores up, thinking people will naturally follow the good example she sets, like the Pied Piper. She misses the blessing of letting God use her to minister to others. See John 21:15–17.

3. *On-the-shelf Mason jar.* This woman at one time participated fully in the Christian life but was hurt along the way. Angry and bitter, tired of "doing all the giving," she has forgotten that while others fail her, if she keeps emptying herself, the Great Husbandman will continually fill her. Eyes off the harvest field, off the good seed, off the cleansing blood, and focused on herself, she may not be aware that she has climbed on a shelf where she gathers dust.

Recently, my husband, an estate planner, called on an eccentric elderly couple with two homes that were overflowing with seventy years of living; a front porch stacked with every *Life* magazine ever printed, all the clothing they, their parents, and their children ever owned. There was chest after chest of beautiful, handmade quilts that had dry rotted. In the cellar were canned

goods dating back twenty-five years. Can you imagine the value of the fruits and vegetables in those jars?

Empty vases can simply sit on a shelf and appreciate in value but all food has a preservation limit. I wonder how many of us are sitting on the shelf? Are we ready to come down and be dusted off? See Matthew 5:14–16.

4. *Filled Mason jar.* This woman, a true, committed Christian, made a conscious decision that she would rather be a Mason jar, year after year cleansed, filled, opened, and emptied. This process is repeated each time she meets a hungry soul. She is filled with "goodies" she planted and picked during her devotional time, and she is ready to share. She knows it is vital for her to keep the lid off so she can pour out God's mercy, forgiveness, comfort, and love. We believe this woman best presents a balanced picture and with proper attention can be as beautiful as a Ming vase while being as useful as a Mason jar. It is an interesting principle in the Christian life that the more we give, the more we receive. God is acutely aware of committed Christians who busy themselves in the work of meeting the needs of others. See Luke 6:38.

5. *Old, scarred, and nicked Mason jars.* This pictures the older Christian woman that Titus 2 speaks of, who empties herself into the lives of younger women, feeding them the truth of God's Word as it pertains to loving their husbands, children, and home. An older Christian who has spent her life consistently being filled and emptied is quite rare. In fact, very old Mason jars are increasing in value and now bring quite a sum at auctions, despite a few nicks.

You may be that older woman, questioning your value to Christ. Don't think because your face is lined with the nicks of time you are less beautiful or valuable. On the contrary, younger women are hungrier than ever before to share the fruit of women who have lived the abundant life in Him and found it satisfying. We older women may need physical balancing, but often show a life of balance. The Scriptures are full of promises concerning fulfillment and fruitfulness for the saint who has walked with the Lord over the years. See Psalm 92:14–15.

6. *New young Mason jars*. These women are just learning of the excitement of being filled with the "treasure" of Christ. They need guidance in how to use the contents of their jars, and instruction on how to keep their vessel clean, uncontaminated, and sparkling with an unmarred testimony. They need to learn balance and are very vulnerable spiritually. Without proper teaching she can literally "die" on the vine spiritually. Solomon warns about the dire consequences of the young not receiving proper instruction:

> He shall die without instruction; and in the greatness of his folly he shall go astray (Prov. 5:23).

7. *Broken Mason jars*. This type of woman represents me in 1975. She started out doing all the right things after accepting the Savior but somewhere got off the track and failed. Have you ever canned something that failed? I have and while it's necessary to throw away the spoiled contents, with proper cleansing the jar can be used again. This woman is unaware that allowing the contaminating bacteria of the evil one to enter her life will spoil her testimony. There are many things she doesn't understand about how much heat or pressure her jar can take. Have you ever dropped a jar and broken it? There is no hope for repairing a real Mason jar. And humanly speaking, after my fall, there wasn't much hope for me. Only God can take His "super-glue" of the Holy Spirit and put us back together again. Because I can't mend cracked jars, I don't preserve foods in them. But God can mend the impossible and He wants to use us again. In fact we hold a certain comforting attraction for other broken jars who need healing.

Our theory is that if we are content to be practical, utilized, emptied, and refilled Mason jars during our brief stay in this spiritually hungry world, Christ will constantly add touches of color, detail, and beauty to our lives. When we are obedient and faithful, our Mason jar actually is transformed into something more beautiful and rare than a Ming vase. Some of us couldn't classify ourselves as Ming vases by any stretch of imagination.

Others seem to be born with every natural asset possible, which could be as big a liability for them as *lack* of beauty may be for a "plain Jane." Both kinds of women tend to look on themselves with strong dislike or false pride.

By keeping their minds on Christ, both are capable of becoming the most beautiful people. We know the world puts a premium on physical beauty, but we are to view life, not from the world's point of view, but God's.

> Favour is deceitful, and beauty is vain: but a woman that feareth the Lord, she shall be praised (Prov. 31:30).

When Mason jars are constantly exposed to light and temperature changes over the years, the vitamin and nutritional content will dwindle. The same goes with our bodies. After awhile the natural process of decay sets in and we must do all we can to preserve health, appearance, and vitality, because we still have a relatively short timetable of usage. We must redeem the time as Colossians 4:5 tells us.

When we think of the body, we can sometimes tell a person's age by whether she thinks first of her looks or health. While we all desire to look as attractive as possible, there is nothing as important as our health. It governs everything we do. It is difficult to speak to a woman of balance in the area of physical beauty if she has a splitting headache or an ulcerated stomach. Later in this book we will see how stress affects the body with just such ailments. You will see in the following chapters how diet and exercise relate to good health. We suggest you find a physician who will become acquainted with you and who will provide proper checkups. Our physical well-being accounts for whether or not we have clear complexions, shiny hair, and good posture.

Our society is certainly more health conscious than ever before in history. As Christians, we should be setting the example for being healthy, well-nourished, and in good physical condition, fit for His service.

Study Questions

1. What does 2 Timothy 3:17 mean to you when it says we may be "perfect, thoroughly furnished"?
2. After reading the descriptions of different vessels, which are you?
3. Which would you like to be?
4. Is the principle of Luke 6:38 working in your life right now?
5. What can you do to make it apply?

Blueprint for the Body

Anyone who takes the time to pick peas, shell the tiny gems, and then can them knows the labor would all be in vain if you neglected to cleanse and sterilize the jar. Sometimes when I bring a can of fruit from the basement, I see the outside of the jar is dusty. Somehow I don't trust the contents until I have washed the jar and lid with hot soapy water before opening. That applies to human vessels, too. People somehow don't trust what we say about our contents if we are not clean and physically balanced by proper cleansing, diet, exercise, and clothing.

Color Me Clean

For years I had to beg, cajole, and bribe my little ones to bathe. After I thought they had bathed and gone to bed, I would sneak in to kiss their shiny little faces—which were attached to dirty necks!

Almost overnight a metamorphosis occurred and they were standing in the shower twice a day, thirty minutes at a time, using all the hot water. While for mothers this is perplexing, think what confusion this bath-a-day woman felt as she listened to a beautiful, dark-haired woman from another culture explain that bathing too often removes protective oils from the skin and promotes illness.

It hasn't been all that many years since Americans lined up on Saturday night to get their weekly bath in a wooden tub. Often in the same water! I'm told "street people" like bag ladies never have the opportunity to bathe, but just add another layer of clothing in the winter and remove it in the summer.

About a year ago we were invited to a party at what I call a Christian "jetset" home. I worried all day about our family fitting in. I made Matt get a haircut, inspected his "planned-casual" look. I tried on one outfit after another before I met my own approval.

The first couple we were introduced to on that warm evening were multimillionaires, and I tried hard to act like the affair was nothing new to me. The beautiful woman was stunning in a loose-fitting but elegant coral designer dress. I took my time examining the dark-haired, trim, tanned woman. I was sure I had seen her thong sandals in a catalog for over $100. As I looked at her feet, I saw something that changed the picture—dirty toenails! Not just dust kicked on, but dirt imbedded in! It is odd how that one flaw spoiled the whole effect for me.

If I was disappointed in that portrayal of wealth by something so minor, it is possible that what seems a slight oversight on my part might just be the one thing that would turn off someone my life should bless. As a vessel carrying the living Lord Jesus, I must do everything in my power to be polished and clean.

An important woman in my life, now deceased, taught me things about the Lord that did not die with her. She was much older than I, and I thought I was poor, until I met her. Other than the few things others gave her, I never saw her wear anything new. But when I think of Nita, into my mind comes this frail little lady, always so clean she squeaked. Her frayed clothing was starched and pressed crisp; her thin, fine hair was neatly pulled back off her shiny forehead. Her contents were pure and her package spotless. There is no reason we can't give forth at least a clean picture.

Hair Hangups

While clean hair is essential, let me say something about style. The mention of hair brings to mind two people. One is a national news correspondent who is not blessed with easy-to-manage hair. She is often out-of-doors giving her story on the evening news. Her fine, limp hair just hangs there detracting from the news. If she had the right cut for her facial shape and her job, plus a dose of spray, maybe I could remember at least part of her news stories. Her message gets lost while I try to fix her hair by osmosis.

The other woman works in a mall. A petite, lovely woman about thirty-seven years old with a 1957 hairstyle. I have never seen a hair out of place because it is so lacquered that if you bumped into her, one of you would have a concussion. It is teased up about one foot and out to the side about two more. I have walked by her several times to see if some great wind was sucking her to the left. Granted she is neat, clean, and well-groomed, but if she were to give a message before a group of women, I guarantee you they would all be thinking about her hairstyle. How did she get it out that far? How long has it stayed that way? Does she sleep standing up? Can her family ever hug her? What kind of hair spray does she use? I'd like to put up wallpaper with it.

Forgive my being facetious, but experts in cosmetology say that, in looking at the total woman, one sees her hair first, then her eyes, then the overall person. It stands to reason we should keep our hair always clean and brushed, in an easy-to-keep style.

One trip to a professional hairdresser may give you some ideas on styles right for your facial shape.

The oval-shaped face is the standard by which other shapes are compared. This shape is easier to arrange with a variety of hairstyles. (See figure 1.)

Figure 1—Oval

Every hairdresser knows that most people don't have the ideal or oval-shaped face, so they are taught to create the oval illusion by the right haircut and style. Reprinted here are the basic facial shapes. They show on the adjacent figure how the hairstyle can change the shape of the face by illusion.

The oblong facial shape is characterized by a long narrow bone structure. Often this shape face is attached to a long, thin neck.

Figure 2—Oblong

Suggestion: A half-bang or soft fringe across the forehead should be accompanied by soft waves or curls in the crown and nape areas.

Figure 3 shows the square-shaped face, characterized by a wide hairline and jawline.

Figure 3—Square

Suggestion: Brushing hair forward and close to the face just below the cheekbones, and softly combing hair off the forehead, creates an oval illusion by adding the appearance of height to the face. When you comb hair on the sides of the face it helps break the wide, straight lines common to the square face.

The heart-shaped face is characterized by a narrow chin and a large wide forehead (often with a widow's peak).

Figure 4—Heart

Suggestion: Hair brought onto the forehead to reduce the area across it will rectify the heart shape. A pageboy style is good for jawlines because hair is close to the head at the eyes, where narrowness is needed, but the hair is somewhat fuller toward the face around the jaw and below and in front of the ear lobes, where width is needed.

Figure 5, the diamond-shaped face, is characterized by a narrow chin, narrow forehead, and wide cheekbones.

Figure 5—Diamond

Suggestion: Fullness or width is needed in the forehead hairline and the lower cheekbone areas to achieve an attractive oval look. Fullness is not needed in the area of the upper cheekbones, so the hair should be styled close to the head there. A bang or fringe will disguise the narrow forehead, and fullness around the jawbone on the face completes the oval illusion.

Figure 6, the round facial shape, is characterized by a wide hairline and fullness at and below the cheekbones. The contour

Figure 6—Round

moves from each cheekbone through the jawline and chin. The person may be overweight, and the neck may appear short.

Suggestion: Setting and combing height in the top and crown sections of the style tends to diminish some of the roundness. Setting and combing the hair close to the head in the side and nape sections also helps.

Figure 7, the pear facial shape, is characterized by a small or narrow forehead and a rather full jawline.

Figure 7—Pear

Suggestion: Setting and combing the hair to add width from eye level through the crown of the head is helpful. Hair in the side and nape sections should be set and combed in a pattern close to the head.

There are cleansers, creams, and astringents in every price range as well as recipes for making your own out of yogurt, lemons, oats, strawberries, and cucumbers. Most dermatologists say that Vaseline rubbed between fingers until softened, then smoothed over a wet face is the best moisturizing treatment for winter and nighttime.

While speaking of a clean face, I also believe women need to use clean makeup. Not too harsh, not too heavy, with colors that become your skin tone, hair coloring, and eyes. Like the Chinese vase, we don't want our paint to detract from the overall picture. A base well-matched to skin tone will cover blemishes and discolorations. Makeup base should not be used to paint our faces a color totally different from the color of our necks. Eye shadow, mascara, eye liner, blush, and lipsticks are to be used as highlighters, bringing out what is already there, much as the sun shining on the curve of a vase brings light to the highest curve.

Another couple of hints from the skin doctor are: Don't tug or pull on your facial skin, especially around the eyes where skin is more delicate; and don't keep an unprotected face in the sun too long unless you are shopping for early wrinkles or skin cancer.

Body Buddies

We are the best buddy our body has, so we need to be good to it. If we were allowed only one $60,000 luxury automobile for our lifetime, it would be foolish to run it for years without having it tuned up, getting the oil changed, and taking other protective measures. Would we let that car sit out in the rain, snow, and sun without protecting it? Of course not, but we are hardly as kind to our bodies. One of the most baffling things is how ignorant we are about our bodies. We must learn to anticipate changes in our bodies at different ages.

Premenstrual tension is a very real problem with most women, and we would be wise not to make major decisions or allow feelings on those days to be a factor in judging our body, soul, and spirit. Recent medical advances are helping physicians to understand and treat PMS, premenstrual syndrome. We can no longer be made to feel guilty about those strange symptoms like depression or craving sweets, as if we brought them on ourselves.

Menopause is another time of change for a woman. It is best to anticipate that part of our lives intelligently, so reading about and discussing menopausal problems is wise. But, just because Aunt Nell had a hard time doesn't mean we will. As we will see later, a woman going into her "fall" years can be most attractive and vital.

Taking our "machine" in for a checkup, tune-up, and weight

check at least once a year is essential. Pap smears and breast examinations can cut down the threat of cancer in the cervix and breast. Between visits to your physician, you should examine your own breasts a few days after your menstrual period. This will help you know what is normal in your own breasts. It is then easier to discover anything unusual, such as new lumps, nipple discharge, puckering, dimpling, or scaly skin. If any of these symptoms are found you should see your doctor.

Be a special buddy to your feet. If the lady with dirty toenails had been a best friend to her feet she would never have let those toes out of her door without a good scrubbing. I have never treated myself to a pedicure, but I hear it is wonderful. The closest thing I've had is an at-home foot-fixer treatment. There are creams which cause dead skin to slough off, pumice stones, and special brushes to finish the job. Soak your feet for thirty minutes in hot, soapy water, then attend to your toenails and cuticles, end with a soothing cream, and your whole body will feel good. In fact, when acupuncture became popular in this country we found that there are pressure points all over your feet that can control pain in other parts of your body. So, take care of those tootsies! Women have been accused for years of cramming their feet in shoes two sizes too small, and I guess we have all been guilty at some time. But truthfully, I don't want that kind of pain, no matter how cute those shoes are! Buy shoes that will be good to your feet, so your feet can be good to the rest of you.

Recently, while watching a news program, I heard about a physician who was conducting an investigation into the use and abuse of the drug diazepam (Valium). He amazed me by saying that it is not used over long periods of time by psychiatric patients as often as it is by patients with back problems. He said many back problems suffered by women would be prevented by correct posture. I watch otherwise attractive women ruin their overall appearance by slumping or giving way to sway and humpbacks. Most women would feel better and look fifteen pounds thinner if they would stand and sit correctly.

Speaking of sitting, the way we handle the body God gave us says quite a bit about the message we want to give others. If we expose more flesh than is modest or carry ourselves in such a way as to flash a red light, saying, "Look at what I've got," we are in a poor position to share the loveliness of the Lord Jesus.

There is something wonderful about a shiny, clean car on a highway filled with dirty cars. In an age of everyone wearing "grungies," it is refreshing to see women who are no strangers to soap and water. It is good to know that the faint essence of perfume is not just a mask for an unclean body. The supply of deodorizers for every area of the body, from mouth to feet, is endless, so there is no excuse for body odor.

Besides the "normal" aspects of keeping your body healthy and externally clean, there are also certain factors which can render your body internally unclean. In Scripture these are called sins against the body:

> Flee fornication. Every sin that a man doeth is without the body; but he that committeth fornication sinneth against his own body (1 Cor. 6:18).

Yes, our body suffers from sexual sins. That can be verified by the epidemic of venereal disease, abortions, and unwanted pregnancies.

Besides the physical perils associated with sexual indiscretion there is also the strong warning from the Lord that nothing is more out of place than a beautiful woman who will not maintain herself in a morally pure fashion (see Prov. 11:22).

Alcohol and drugs are also enemies of our body. You can look into the watery, blurred eyes of a person whose nose and face is etched with broken veins and tell that person has probably done irreparable damage to the hidden inward parts of his body also.

Study Questions

1. After studying the basic facial shapes, which one are you?
2. How could you change your hairstyle to give the illusion of an oval shape?

3. How does the way we carry our body give messages about us?
4. We usually plan to bathe and brush our teeth daily. What can we do to plan to stay internally clean?

Chapter 3
Feeding the Body

Culinary Confessions

Dan Bennet said, "Probably nothing in the world arouses more false hope than the first four hours of a diet."

The sad-eyed young woman before me hated herself to the point of suicide because all she thought of was food.

After a tiring weekend of speaking at a retreat in the Smoky Mountains, I had been followed to my room by a mother, worried and undeterred by my busy schedule, determined I should talk to her daughter. While I would rather the daughter herself say, "I need help," the mother's persistence left me with no alternative, so I listened to the sixteen-year-old girl in my disarrayed hotel room.

As I listened, I was aware of similarities between her story and mine. I too was being obsessed with food. I no sooner finished lunch than I thought of dinner. But there the similarity ended. I saw a young woman of average height who weighed less than eighty pounds and who stuck her finger down her throat whenever she *did* eat a normal meal, which was seldom. She was my first encounter with anorexia nervosa and bulimia. She was under psychiatric care, and I certainly didn't want to meddle in an area that required treatment professionally.

I shared with the girl that God did love her and made her body to last for a certain amount of time. If she didn't properly care for it she was actually destroying His work. I encouraged her to believe she could get well, and I shared a few things about renewing her mind (covered in another chapter). I encouraged her to continue with professional counseling because it often takes months and even years to cure.

While I talked to that tiny, auburn-haired young lady, I couldn't help wondering, "If she thinks eighty pounds is fat, I wonder what she thinks of me?"

I was thirty pounds overweight, and I too was miserable. I hated my lack of discipline and self-control. But whose sin was greater? Whether we eat too much or too little or the wrong things, we sin against the body God has given us. It is our packaging for the Lord Jesus.

Have you ever bought a nice gift for someone, only to pick up a flimsy gift box that will not stand up at the corners? Or have you ever had to put a small gift in a huge box, or vice versa? We want a box that suits our gift. By the same token, we must not only look at our body as a one-of-a-kind, but as the showcase for our Savior.

Lest this all become too heavy, let me assure you that I have a real struggle with my weight. One of the clues that shows I'm in trouble is that snoring *never* gets on *my* nerves; it is my signal that the house is asleep and I can sneak out of the bedroom, close the door, and streak to the kitchen to have an affair with the love of my life—FOOD!

While Snickers is my favorite, I know that the real monkey on my back is any kind of sweets. I prefer chocolate, but when I need a fix, anything with sugar will do. Is there any hope for a person like me? Yes! Three things happened that pushed me onto the right track. 1) I became a grandmother; 2) I looked in the mirror and saw that I was a typical, old-fashioned, fat, matronly grandmother; 3) I looked at a photo of me holding the new baby and I didn't like what I saw.

Another realization showed me the seriousness of my problem: If I was filled with the Holy Spirit, it would be evidenced by the fruit of self-control. Wham! That hit me hard. The battle was in my mind and I had a choice to make: Obey or give in and settle for what I had become. I decided to enroll in a weight loss class and was pleasantly surprised with the results. I know now that I will have to count calories for the rest of my life. I don't like it, but that's the way it is.

Ultimately we must stay fit for the Lord. During my dumpy, dowdy period I loved to quote: "For the Lord seeth not as man seeth: for man looketh on the outward appearance, but the Lord looketh on the heart" and "pass me another cookie" in the same breath. We can all find Scripture to back up whatever we want to do. The trouble with that verse is that, while it is true that God sees the heart, man *does* see the package.

I think we must weigh Scripture with *medical* evidence that obesity shortens the life span and with *psychological* evidence that self-esteem diminishes as weight increases, and then lose weight for God, ourselves, and those who see the package.

In this area, we need to strive more for the Ming vase look. We must:

1. Do it so we will live longer.
2. Do it as an example of self-control for our family.
3. Do it so our husbands have to catch their breath to whistle.
4. Do it so our children are proud of their mothers.

It is difficult to tell children not to indulge in drugs or drinking if we are overeating.

Finally, do it because nothing is too good for the creation of the Lord. Proverbs 23:1–3 tells us:

When thou sittest to eat with a ruler, consider diligently what is before thee: and put a knife to thy throat, if thou be a man given to appetite. Be not desirous of his dainties: for they are deceitful meat.

I don't consider myself rich, but while I don't eat huge portions, I am intrigued by dainties which are deceitful. Sugar satisfies my sweet tooth and makes me temporarily happy, but the calories are empty. Not only does it do nothing to benefit my body, in large amounts it is harmful. The healthy way to fill a sweet tooth is with fruit.

There are many alternatives to choose from when considering dieting. However, care must be taken in choosing a diet that is best for you. The ends *do not* justify the means if you end up with a calcium deficiency or low blood sugar. We believe it is better to avoid crash diets and lose slowly. We need to learn something about the food the body needs, and let that knowledge control our eating habits.

Let us share a plan that *will work* if you work at it.

The Thirty Day Way

What follows is a suggested plan by which you can lose either one pound per week, two pounds per week, or three pounds per week over a one-month period of time. The first step in The Thirty Day Way plan is to calculate the number of calories that you are required to consume each day to maintain your current body weight. To do this, fill in the blank below marked *present weight*. Then multiply your present weight by fifteen to arrive at your daily calorie intake which maintains your present weight.

Next, fill in your daily maintenance total in one of the three columns below depending on whether you want to arrive at a daily calorie intake to lose one pound per week, two pounds per week, or three pounds per week. After making the appropriate subtractions you will find at the bottom of the column that you have chosen the amount of calories a day that you should consume in order to lose the pounds per week that you wish.

```
┌─────────────┐                    ┌─────────────┐
│             │      × 15 =        │             │
│             │                    │             │
└─────────────┘                    └─────────────┘
Your present weight                 The number of calo-
                                    ries necessary each
                                    day to maintain your
                                    present weight. This
                                    is referred to as your
                                    Daily Maintenance
                                    Total.
```

Enter your Daily   Enter your Daily   Enter your Daily
Maintenance Total   Maintenance Total   Maintenance Total
here   here   here

_____   _____   _____
        −500   −1000   −1500
Your   →_____   Your   →_____   Your   →_____
calorie intake   calorie intake   calorie intake
per day to   per day to   per day to
lose 1 lb/week   lose 2 lbs/   lose 3 lbs/
                          week   week

The next step is to divide your number of daily calories into three portions using the chart below.

Your chosen daily   Your chosen daily   Your chosen daily
total calorie intake   total calorie intake   total calorie intake

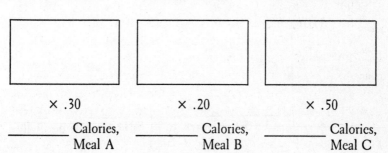

```
┌───────────┐      ┌───────────┐      ┌───────────┐
│           │      │           │      │           │
│           │      │           │      │           │
└───────────┘      └───────────┘      └───────────┘
    × .30              × .20              × .50
_____ Calories,   _____ Calories,   _____ Calories,
       Meal A             Meal B             Meal C
```

Meal A, meal B, and meal C are the three meals which you will eat each day. Individuals are so different concerning which meals are easiest for them to go "light" on calories and which meals they are likely to go "heavy" on calories, that we have found it most effective to allow each individual to decide when they will eat their meal A, meal B, and meal C each day. For most, meal C will be the supper meal, meal A will often be the breakfast meal, and meal B will be lunch. This may not, however, be the most effective for you and you can experiment with shifting the meals around until you find the pattern which most serves your ability to stay on the diet. Once you have decided the sequence of meals, for example, meal A at breakfast, meal B at lunch, and meal C at supper, then designate which meal you will be eating at the various times of the day on the *Weekly Food Program*. For each meal on the food program you will have an allowed calorie limit. Using any one of the many calorie counting books available in most supermarkets, bookstores, or department stores, fill in a selection of foods so as not to exceed the allowed calories for each meal. You will notice that on the left-hand side of the daily food program sheet is a column giving the suggested types of food to make up each meal.

A word about plateaus. Every person who has dieted knows that there are plateau periods (even brief gain periods) when their weight ceases to drop. Don't get discouraged! These plateaus are part of your body's normal physiological adjustment to a new metabolic pace. Below is a chart showing in the dotted line a

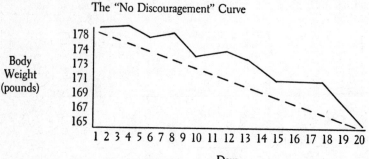

The "No Discouragement" Curve

Body Weight (pounds)

Days

Week of _____   30 DAY WAY   CALORIE LIMIT PER DAY _____

WEEKLY FOOD PROGRAM

SUGGESTED FOOD GROUPS	MON.	TUE.	WED.	THUR.	FRI.	SAT.	SUN.
MORNING MEAL (SUGGESTED FOODS) Fruit serving Egg or Cheese Cereal with ½ cup milk Bread Beverage	Meal ___ Allowed calories for this meal ___ Foods:	Meal ___ Allowed calories for this meal ___ Foods:	Meal ___ Allowed calories for this meal ___ Foods:	Meal ___ Allowed calories for this meal ___ Foods:	Meal ___ Allowed calories for this meal ___ Foods:	Meal ___ Allowed calories for this meal ___ Foods:	Meal ___ Allowed calories for this meal ___ Foods:
NOON MEAL (SUGGESTED FOODS) Poultry, Meat or Fish or Eggs or Cheese Vegetable (1) Bread (if desired) Beverage	Meal ___ Allowed calories for this meal ___ Foods:	Meal ___ Allowed calories for this meal ___ Foods:	Meal ___ Allowed calories for this meal ___ Foods:	Meal ___ Allowed calories for this meal ___ Foods:	Meal ___ Allowed calories for this meal ___ Foods:	Meal ___ Allowed calories for this meal ___ Foods:	Meal ___ Allowed calories for this meal ___ Foods:
EVENING MEAL (SUGGESTED FOODS) Poultry, Meat or Fish Vegetables (2) Bread (if not eaten at Noon meal) Beverage	Meal ___ Allowed calories for this meal ___ Foods:	Meal ___ Allowed calories for this meal ___ Foods:	Meal ___ Allowed calories for this meal ___ Foods:	Meal ___ Allowed calories for this meal ___ Foods:	Meal ___ Allowed calories for this meal ___ Foods:	Meal ___ Allowed calories for this meal ___ Foods:	Meal ___ Allowed calories for this meal ___ Foods:

41

theoretically "ideal" course of weight loss on a diet. The solid line is the actual weight loss of a real person on the diet. (Both lines reach the same end at about the same time!)

What about Vitamins and Minerals?*

The issue of proper consumption of vitamins and minerals often comes up concerning the matter of weight reduction through dietary restrictions of food intake. For the most part, common sense can be relied upon in ascertaining the proper use of vitamin and mineral supplements. Your local pharmacy or health food store will carry several brands of high potency multivitamin and mineral supplements. One of these a day will suffice in all normal situations in giving you plenty of the body's daily essential vitamins and minerals. The only two vitamins which I will occasionally recommend in extra doses are vitamin C (in a dose of approximately 500 mg per day) and a single capsule B-Complex daily to provide extra levels of the essential B vitamin group.

What about Cancer?

One of the most exciting recent advances in understanding nutrition has come in the area of a new appreciation for the protective role which certain food groups can play in the prevention of cancer. Some of the potential cancers are mentioned along with foods, as well as other substances, which tend to *increase* and *decrease* your risk of cancer in particular areas of the body in the following table:

Cancer Site	Foods and Substances That Will Increase Your Cancer Risk	Foods and Substances That Will Decrease Your Cancer Risk
Esophagus	*Excessive alcohol, especially in smokers *Nitrite-pickled foods, e.g. pickled vegetables	*All Fresh Fruits and Vegetables
Stomach	*Wood smoked foods; smoked hams, smoked fish *Nitrite-cured meats, e.g. frankfurters, bologna, bacon	*Raw green or yellow vegetables, especially lettuce *Vegetables of the cabbage family, e.g. cabbage, broccoli *Foods high in Vitamin C
Colon and Rectum	*Animal or vegetable fats (e.g. fatty cuts of meat, whole dairy products, cooking oils, cooking fats)	*High fiber foods, especially whole grain cereals and flours *Fresh fruits and vegetables *Foods in the cabbage family, including cabbage, broccoli, cauliflower, brussels sprouts, and kale

(continued)

Cancer Site	Foods and Substances That Will Increase Your Cancer Risk	Foods and Substances That Will Decrease Your Cancer Risk
Liver	*Excessive alcohol consumption (this can cause liver cirrhosis, which increases the risk of cancer of the liver)	*Low alcohol consumption *A well-balanced diet
Lung	*Tobacco smoking (major cause) *Diet low in carotene or Vitamin A	*Diminished tobacco smoking *A balanced diet containing Vitamins A & C, and fresh vegetables; particularly cabbage family (see above) and those foods rich in carotene: spinach, pumpkin, carrots, sweet potatoes, tomatoes, cantaloupes, apricots, peaches
Bladder	*Heavy use of saccharin containing foods, e.g. diet soft drinks *Tobacco smoking adds to this risk	*A well-balanced diet with Vitamin A and Vitamin C rich foods, preferably fresh

Cancer Site	Foods and Substances That Will Increase Your Cancer Risk	Foods and Substances That Will Decrease Your Cancer Risk
Reproductive System (especially breast and prostate)	*Animal and vegetable fats	*Well-balanced diet with low fat intake

Study Questions

1. Which fruit of the Spirit should be evidenced when food is served?
2. Do you have a particular food that causes problems for you: Are you willing to share this with the class?
3. If you recognize yourself as a compulsive overeater, can you acknowledge your helplessness to God and ask for His help?
4. Could you make a commitment with another person in the group to try the Thirty-Day Way if you are overweight?
5. If you are not overweight would you commit yourself to prayer for an overweight sister for 30 days?

Chapter 4
Exercising the Body

Let's Go Wogging

"Bodily exercise profiteth little so hand me the potato chips!" I was tempted to scream this at that peppy little Richard Simmons as he jumped hyperactively around on my TV screen. However, I knew he had a point when he talked about the need for exercise all of our lives—it isn't just for the young. I knew because, even though I was losing weight, nothing seemed to look like it used to. Every physical attribute was shifting downward and forward. Gravity!

As I searched for the miraculous one-piece undergarment to squeeze it all away, I became discouraged. It only squeezed it all upward. It reminded me of Jane Russell's "advice to full-figured gals."

It seemed I had done everything to avoid exercise. Then one cold winter day I felt that even the Lord was looking at me with disdain. I listened to interviews with svelte stars who proclaimed the wonders of jogging, and I decided to bring my body under subjection. After four days of punishment, I felt like writing to those stars:

> Dear Jogging Enthusiast: Where is the *high* I'm supposed to achieve? I just returned from my fourth day of jogging and I'm at an all-time low. If I could catch my breath I would sob. As it is, the tears are frozen to my face and I feel like I don't have long to live. The calves of my legs are having labor pains and I *know* what they will give birth to—charley horses! Are ladies really supposed to sweat this way?

By the way, jogging fans, where do you get those cute little running suits for less than the price of a VW Rabbit?

There's much more, but lucky for me, I can take out most of my frustration at my typewriter. However, I didn't give up and after a couple of months of consistent mile-and-a-half-per-day walking and running, I was surprised by a firmer, healthier body. No longer did one flight of stairs leave me breathing hard. The pride I felt was not at how I looked, but because I accepted the challenge and won. Exercise is more than a beauty aid. It strengthens the heart muscle, helps circulation, keeps other muscles working, keeps complexions clear and healthy, and gives you a good feeling about yourself. This kind of exercise is referred to as *aerobic* as it improves the efficiency and endurance of the cardio-vascular system. This does not happen overnight so be patient, persevere, and eventually you'll find yourself doing more with less effort.

In addition to that, aerobics help you shed inches and pounds, firm and tone, and generally increase your level of personal well-being, physically and mentally.

Wogging Your Way to Fitness

What is Wogging anyway? Wogging is a form of aerobic exercise specifically designed for women that combines walking and jogging. The reason for Wogging as an exercise form is that it offers the best of both walking and jogging. Walking has the advantage of being initially less rigorous, allowing a progressive building of physical fitness. Jogging adds the additional quality of developing a more intense level of fitness. In Wogging, you walk until you are warmed up, then you jog until you are moderately winded then you go back to walking until you are comfortable and then begin jogging again. The sequence continues until you finish the assigned distance.

The first step in beginning the Wogging exercise program is to determine your level of physical fitness. This is done as follows:

Choose a reasonably pleasant day and dress out in exercise clothing. Take a watch with a second hand along with you, and set out on a local street to cover as much ground as you can by walking and jogging in a time period of twelve minutes. You can walk and/or jog; if you get winded, slow down for a while until you get your breath, and then pick up the pace again. At the end of exactly twelve minutes, mark how far you've gotten. (You may need to go back and measure the stretch you've covered in your automobile on the odometer.) Place the distance you covered in the box below labeled as miles covered in 12 minutes.

Then, look up your Age Quotient in the following table and place it in the box below. Multiply miles covered by Age Quotient to arrive at your Stamina Total. Place your Stamina Total in the appropriate blank. After determining your fitness level, follow the Wogging fitness program that is right for you.

Your Age	Your Age Quotient	Your Age	Your Age Quotient
Age 17–29	100	37	108
30	101	38	109
31	102	39	110
32	103	40	111
33	104	41	112
34	105	42	113
35	106	43	114
36	107	44	115

45	116	54	125
46	117	55	126
47	118	56	127
48	119	57	128
49	120	58	129
50	121	59 and over	130
51	122		
52	123		
53	124		

$$\boxed{} \times \boxed{} = \boxed{}$$

Miles covered in 12 minutes	Your Age Quotient	Your Stamina Total

Under 120	121–140	141–170	Over 171
Your beginning fitness level is POOR	Your beginning fitness level is FAIR	Your beginning fitness level is GOOD	Your beginning fitness level is EXCELLENT

If your beginning fitness level is POOR, then your Wogging fitness program will extend over a period of 24 weeks.

Week Number	Frequency per Week	Distance	Time Requirement
1–4	4	1 mile	15 minutes
5–8	4	1.5	20 minutes
9–12	4	2.0	25 minutes
13–16	4	2.5	30 minutes

| 17–20 | 4 | 3.0 | 35 minutes |
| 21–24 | 4 | 3.0 | 30 minutes |

If your beginning fitness level is FAIR, then your Wogging fitness program will extend over a period of 22 weeks.

Week Number	Frequency per Week	Distance	Time Requirement
1–3	4	1 mile	15 minutes
4–6	4	1.5	20 minutes
7–10	4	2.0	25 minutes
11–14	4	2.5	30 minutes
15–18	4	3.0	35 minutes
19–22	4	3.0	30 minutes

If your beginning fitness level is GOOD, then your Wogging fitness program will extend over a period of 20 weeks.

Week Number	Frequency per Week	Distance	Time Requirement
1–3	4	1 mile	15 minutes
4–6	4	1.5	20 minutes
7–9	4	2.0	25 minutes
10–12	4	2.5	30 minutes
13–16	4	3.0	35 minutes
17–20	4	3.0	30 minutes

If your beginning fitness level is EXCELLENT, then your Wogging fitness program will extend over a period of 18 weeks.

Week Number	Frequency per Week	Distance	Time Requirement
1–3	4	1 mile	15 minutes
4–6	4	1.5	20 minutes

7–9	4	2.0	25 minutes
10–12	4	2.5	30 minutes
13–15	4	3.0	35 minutes
16–18	4	3.0	30 minutes

"Three" to Get Ready

The following are three simple warm-up exercises which will serve to gently stretch out the muscles of your legs and lower torso prior to your Wogging program each day.

TWISTERS

Start by standing with your feet apart about 30 inches. Put your arms straight out and twist the trunk all the way to the right, then all the way to the left. Repeat this 10–20 times smoothly until it is no longer uncomfortable.

CIRCLE-TOUCHES

Standing with your feet apart about 30 inches, place your hands together over your head and then with both hands together touch the inside of your left foot, the ground between your two feet and then the inside of your right foot, and then return to an erect position. Repeat this 10–20 times until it is no longer difficult.

THE SPRINTER

First assume a squatting position with your hands flat on the ground, then extend one leg as far back as possible. Hold that position momentarily and then extend the other leg while bringing the first leg back up to its original position. Repeat the process 10–20 times until it is no longer difficult.

Contraindications

These are physical conditions which may prevent you from engaging in this fitness program, and you need to consult your physician if you suffer from any of these.

1. A recent heart attack. Medical experts recommend that you wait at least three to four months after a heart attack before beginning a regular exercise program, and even then your program must be closely supervised by your doctor.
2. Any kind of on-going disease of the heart, including diseases of the heart valves such as with rheumatic fever damage, any

congenital heart disease which limits heart function, or an enlarged heart (as in congestive heart failure).

3. Severe irregularities of heartbeat which require medical attention.

4. Diabetes which is severe and not under good control, that is, with blood sugars fluctuating from too little to too much sugar in the blood daily.

5. Excessive obesity. If you are fifty to sixty pounds overweight, you need to consult your physician to be sure that you are physically capable of beginning and continuing a graduated exercise program.

6. High blood pressure which is not well controlled by medication. A suggested cut off for this would be if your blood pressure is at or greater than 160 (systolic) or 110 (diastolic).

7. If you are suffering from an infectious disease and are still in the acute or active phase of the illness, you should not enter into the program until you have recovered. If you develop an infectious illness during the Wogging exercise program, it is best to cease the program until your body has had time to recover from the infection and return to good health. You can restart the program at a level slightly below when you stopped.

8. Any chronic diseases such as a history of chronic kidney disease; anemia which is under treatment, but not yet corrected; chronic lung disease; arthritis in the back, legs, feet, or ankles which is requiring medical treatment; convulsive diseases such as epileptic seizures which are not completely controlled; insulin-dependent diabetes; blood vessel disease of the legs which has produced decreased circulation; or any chronic medical problem for which you are receiving care from a physician.

Study Questions

1. Discuss with the group the form of exercise you are involved in and how it makes you feel.

2. If our "body is the temple of the Holy Spirit," should we be involved in an exercise program?
3. Discuss benefits of exercise for your mind and body.
4. If you are not involved in a program will you commit yourself to thirty days of Wogging?

Chapter 5
Clothing the Body

Cluttered Closets and Calico Lids

Do you ever wonder why some women always look all put together, just right for the occasion, while you look like you just didn't have time? It definitely does take time and thought.

Last Valentine's Day my friend Bonnie gave me a cute little squatty Mason jar full of red candies with an "I love you" cross-stitched lid cover. It was decorated with a red and white dotted ribbon. What a joy that little jar brings me. I took a clue from her, and when I made plum jelly last summer, I took some green calico left over from my ruffled kitchen curtains and made ruffled covers for some of the jar lids. It took a little time and thought, as well as material, but the jars added a quaint, colorful touch to the shelf under my kitchen window. They cheer me by reminding me that I am not only created, but I have been loaned some creativity of my own. You can be sure I didn't cart Bonnie's jar or my calico-dressed jars to the basement. They were dressed for a kitchen party, not basement drudgery; they had the services of an exterior decorator! As I watch women of every age, shape, and economic level go to the grocery in dresses meant for lawn parties, I want to scream. When I go into an office where a lovely secretary wears a low-cut, hip-high-slit dress meant for cocktail parties, I want to scream. When I see a huge human wearing tight-fitting knit pants and a T-shirt to a symphony, I want to scream:

Help! Exterior decorator needed!

An interior decorator comes to a home first to look at the size and shape of the rooms before thinking about what to put in them. Just so, women need to take a good look in the mirror at their size and shape before deciding what to put on.

If we are under five feet seven inches tall and weigh one ounce over 125 pounds, I doubt seriously if we need to wear a one-piece sweater dress. Or, if we are five feet tall and weigh 195 pounds, we definitely don't want to wear broad horizontal stripes.

Take a little time, go to a really nice shop and try on different styles until finding one that looks best. Don't buy anything just because you like *it*—you must look nice *in it!*

Like most women, I have defects. About twenty years ago I did what I just recommended. We were a family of five, on a strict budget, and I was still wearing clothes from high school. I dressed up one day, went to downtown Louisville and waltzed into dress shops I couldn't afford. They didn't know that, and I tried on expensive clothes as though I could buy anything I wanted. I made some interesting discoveries. My main defects, big hips and a not-too-tight tummy, could be hidden by wearing jacket dresses, tunic tops, or a blazer. Since that time, only a select few have ever seen me without a jacket. I have left instructions to bury me in a blazer. I began, after that, to collect blazers when they were on sale. Because they are a good investment for any time, I can buy wool ones in the spring and summer ones in the fall for up to 75 percent off the normal price. You can get good-quality blazers for bargain store prices.

Now, don't rush out to buy blazers if you are built too close to the floor. Let's look at a few ways to hide defects with proper style, from a notebook I compiled from magazine articles, TV shows, and my own discoveries.

Small Body

If you are under five feet three inches tall, you need to concentrate on long-linear design and simplicity. You look nice in pleated skirts with sharp vertical lines. You can gain height by wearing one color, head to toe, with different tones for interest. Try to accentuate a long line from waist to feet. You can wear medium-width belts, subtle vertical stripes, and fitted jackets. There are some things that don't become you, such as horizontal stripes, loosely draped garments, or wild, large prints. Fancy lace and frills, bulky fabrics (thick knotty wools), and big furs or too many colors tend to shorten you. A silky two-piece dress in a small print with long sleeves is ideal for the petite figure.

Small Hips

You can wear things I wouldn't be caught dead in, and I'm jealous! You can wear full skirts, culottes, and pleated or dirndl skirts. Flapper-style loose dresses and loose pleats give the illusion of more hips. You can wear substantial-weight fabrics and overshirts. Tight skirts or badly cut, tight slacks are not a good look for you.

Large Hips

Your best bets are skirts that hug the top of your hips and fall gently, in simple designs, and either darker than the tops or the same color. Use substantial-weight fabrics for straight-line tunic tops that end at the bottom of the sleeve of your jacket. Blazers and jackets are good for you unless your arms are too heavy. Focus attention on the upper body with color, scarves, or jewelry. Things I dare not wear include large plaids, broad horizontal stripes, skirts in loud colors or with excess pleats or gathering at the hips. Some fabrics to stay away from are wide-wale corduroy, lightweight jersey fabrics that cling, and sweater knits. Dirndl skirts are darling but not for you. If you are blessed with ample thighs and buttocks these tips are also for you.

Short Torso

You too look nice in overblouses, sweaters worn over skirts, jackets, and tunic tops. Don't wear wide belts, very short jackets, skirts with wide waistbands, or belted tunics. A dropped-waist, loose-fitting dress disguises a short torso.

Long Torso

Looks best in skirts hemmed just below the knee, wide belts, and vests. You can really get away with the layered, separate look, but be careful about short hemlines and belts worn low on the hips. You are one of the few who can wear horizontal stripes with a wide belt.

Narrow Shoulders

What if your problem is narrow shoulders? You will look wonderful in padded shoulders. You look best in shirts with set-in sleeves with either small collars, V-necks or boat necks. You can also wear dropped shoulders, but beware of full-cut big tops, turtlenecks, bulky fabrics, and large coats and jackets. Raglan sleeves minimize broad shoulders, but padded and leg-o'-mutton sleeves can be worn to advantage by the woman with narrow shoulders. A risk for *broad shoulders* are cap and puff sleeves, padded shoulders, broad horizontal stripes, or boat necks. She can, however, wear full coats, dolman sleeves, V-necks and drop shoulders.

Full Bust

I don't know whether to consider myself blessed by a full bust to sit atop my full hips or not, but like others, I must watch dolman sleeves, tight knits in either blouses or dresses, and patch pockets on skirts or dresses. I don't need to wear clinging fabrics, puffy sleeves, or light-weight fabrics that reveal bra lines. The princess line is not for us. We look best in open collars, V-necks, and loose tops. I love to collect silk shirts on sale. A suit with a collarless cardigan and a vertical-striped shirt plays down a full bust.

Small Bust

The small-busted woman has very few restrictions unless she is full-hipped, then she looks best in easy, flowing blouses. She is the perfect candidate for a blouse with a tiered yoke.

Thick Waist

For a thick waist it is best to steer away from nipped-in waists, wide or wrap belts, and skirts that pleat or gather at the waist. You look best in blouson-style shirts and dresses, unfitted jackets, vests, and loose waistlines. Focus attention away from your waist.

Small Waist

If you are blessed with a small waist, by all means don't hide it with blouson styles, unbelted tunic tops, or shapeless dresses. I wouldn't even wear a vest if it covered the size of your waist. Show it off with nipped-in waists or interesting belts. A tie at the waist emphasizes the plus of a small waist.

Short and Long Necks

What if your problem is a short neck? Wear open collars, V-necks, tapered hairstyles, and scoop necks. You shorten the appearance of your neck further by heavy, bulky scarves, turtlenecks, high collars, or mandarin or jewel neck collars. Even the classic T-shirt is not for you. Just the opposite is true if your neck is too long. Perhaps none of these is your particular trouble spot. A sales person in a nice department store will be glad to help you find "your" look. Some questions for Christian women to ask themselves while shopping for clothes: Is it decent or modest? Is it attractive on me? Will it last more than one season? Is it good quality? Is it within my budget?

My friends used to tease me about my "beige period" because I always seemed to gravitate to creams through camels and browns. Since all the new information about skin tones is out, I find that because of my particular coloring, the autumn shades look best on me. I used to think those colors looked best because of my green eyes and light brown hair. But, it is the *skin tone* that determines what group of colors looks *best* on us. In makeup, the coral-to-orange family of colors is also good for me. One of my friends always goes for pastels. I have never liked them on me, but she is a summer person, and they do look best on her. One of the books covering this subject is called *Color Me Beautiful* by Carole Jackson, and if you are not sure about which colors suit you best, I suggest you buy a copy or check out one from the library.

For as long as I can remember, our money has gone into raising and educating our four children. There never seemed to be any money left for me. For years I only wore clothing that had been given to me. I even tried making clothes, but since I don't sew that was a disaster. A few years ago, I stumbled onto a system that keeps me well-dressed on a fraction of what most people spend. When my last child entered school nine years ago I found if I left an hour early to pick up the children, I could browse through a store or two, just looking. I wasn't in the market for anything. There are racks and out-of-the-way corners in nearly every store where they place items that didn't sell in the clearance sale or that have minor defects. Sometimes in the midst of remnants is a jewel, a blazer that someone has returned, a beautiful blouse that was overlooked, or just something the Lord left in the field of just-picked goodies for me to glean. All it really takes is time and a prayer for

God to help you find what He wants you to wear. I make a regular junket to the very expensive shops *after* the regular Fourth of July and January clearance sales. Things may be picked over, but if you are careful, you may find a treasure. Recently a store in our town began a 75 percent off sale in the designer department at the end of each season. I purchased my best outfits there at a price I would pay at a discount store. Pray that God will make you a wise shopper. If He even counts the hair on our heads, doesn't it make sense that He cares about what we wear?

Study Questions

1. Discuss with the group your honest assessment of what your body type is, your height, weight, and figure problems.
2. What are five guidelines Christian women should follow when shopping for clothes?
3. Share with the group the basic style that is most attractive on you. Is it alright if they disagree with you? Are you open to change?
4. List ways you can shop on a budget and still look up-to-date and attractive.

Chapter 6
Restoring the Body

Depression, PMS, and Other Imbalancers

When Christ said in Matthew 18 that He came to save (or restore) that which was lost, He meant that He intended to put in proper balance every aspect of the human life. Accordingly, He restored people on each of the three levels of human functioning:

1. On the physical level—by a return to biological balance and health;
2. On the emotional level—by a return to well-being and self-esteem within the personality;
3. On the spiritual level—by a return to fellowship with God through salvation and restored spiritual power.

Restoration on the emotional and spiritual levels will be discussed in Chapters 12 and 18 respectively.

Restoring Balance on the Physical Level (the Brain or Mind)

The health and proper functioning of your mind (or brain) is your most important health concern, for although medical science may be able to transplant hearts, livers, and lungs, there is no such thing as a brain transplant. What you've got is what you'll have for the rest of your life, so the delicate fine tuning of the brain's internal hormones (neurotransmitters) is very crucial to your good mental health. These neurotransmitters are truly the body's chemicals that restore.

Fortunately, the Lord has equipped our brains to maintain a proper balance of internal hormones (neurotransmitters) in almost every circumstance. It is only when this vital balance is upset by some significant intervening event, disease, injury, or inborn defect that we see the symptoms of mental illness (or the so-called "nervous breakdown"). Such chemical imbalances within the brain are the only true forms of mental illness, since they have their origin in the physical functioning of the mind. On the other hand, those emotional problems which arise from inner conflicts within the personality or from self-defeating patterns of behavior developed from childhood experiences are best thought of as being on the psychological level of functioning. And those problems which are the result of unbiblical decisions or priorities are located on the spiritual level. We will look at both the problems of the psychological level and the spiritual level in the following chapters. But let us now turn our attention toward the mind's physical level of functioning and the chemical and structural balances and imbalances which are so crucial to its proper operation.

There are many ways to approach the categorizing of the different chemical and structural imbalances which can disrupt the normal functioning of the brain (mind). I have grouped these "imbalancers" into five categories. An indepth study of these is beyond the scope of our purposes in this book; however, we will look briefly at each of these five major imbalancers and point out the predominant causes, symptoms, and treatments of each. These five imbalancers are:

I. Depression
II. Dementia
III. Damage to the brain
IV. Disintegration of rational thinking (schizophrenia)
V. Delusional mania

In the following pages Dr. Byrd talks extensively about depression and how it can affect the physical well-being of Christian women, even to the point of inducing many physical disorders like migraine headaches, ulcers, colitis, arthritis, low back pain, and sleep and eating disorders.

Depression

According to recent estimates, approximately one out of twenty Americans is medically diagnosed as suffering from depression, and considering the many more who do not seek formal treatment, it is conservatively estimated that more than twenty million Americans suffer from this major health problem. Depression occurs twice as often in women as it does in men and seems to reach its peak in individuals in their forties and fifties. Depression is no respecter of socioeconomic status; in fact, affluency often seems to be associated with depression.

But what is depression? Depression is best defined as an internal sense of loss, sometimes manifested primarily by emotional despondency and other times primarily by physical symptoms. *Depression* is a popular word today. People casually remark, "Boy, I'm depressed." But, depression is more than feeling low over a set of events. Depression is a serious health problem manifested by a mood state of intense despondency.

Depression is also among the most painful of medical disorders. In Psalm 102:3–7 David described depression as follows:

> For my days have been consumed in smoke, and my bones are burned as an hearth. My heart is smitten, and withered like grass; so that I

forget to eat my bread. By reason of the voice of my groaning my bones cleave to my skin. I am like a pelican of the wilderness: like an owl of the desert. I watch, and am as a sparrow alone upon the house top.

Because of the intense suffering associated with a severe depression, suicide is unfortunately the solution which some individuals choose to end the pain of depression. Suicide is the tenth leading cause of death in the United States, and, in fact, 10 percent of individuals who make a suicidal gesture eventually will die of suicide from another attempt. Suicide threats must be taken seriously because 80 percent of those individuals who commit suicide have warned someone previously concerning their intentions. Women attempt suicide five times more often than men, although they are less likely to die from their suicide attempt due to their usual choice of a less violent means. In an individual who is depressed, the following factors would tend to make suicide a more likely possibility.

1. Forty years old or older.
2. Separated, divorced, or widowed.
3. Unemployed or retired and living alone.
4. Poor health with an acute or chronic medical condition having developed in the preceding six months.
5. A history of nervous or mental disorders, usually depressions in the past and often either alcohol or drug abuse.
6. A tendency towards impulsive actions and willingness to consider using a more violent method of suicide (for example, hanging, firearms, jumping).
7. Often there is extensive preparation for the suicidal attempt with the leaving of a note, preparing of a will, giving away valuable personal items.

If there is any positive side to depression, it is the fact that depression is one of the most treatable of all mental illnesses. With the recent increase in research and development of new pharmacological treatments for depression, most physical depressions, which have at their base a chemical imbalance in the mind, can be treated by one or more of the new antidepressants with good success. Some of the most well known of these antidepressant medications include Elavil, Tofranil, Sinequan, Norpramin, Triavil, and Desyrel. There are many others, and the prescription and use of these requires the supervision of a skilled general physician or a psychiatrist.

Symptoms of Depression

Depression can present itself in a variety of seemingly unrelated ways. The symptoms of depression may be divided into five categories: 1) Sadness of mood. 2) Confusion (sometimes manifested by having difficulty concentrating, poor memory, or what is described as "painful thinking"). 3) Physical symptoms. 4) Anxiety. 5) Psychosis.

Sadness of mood. The overwhelming feeling of sadness or despair is probably the most common symptom of depression. Depressed individuals may often cry or at least feel like crying and internally they will describe feelings of fatigue, discouragement, and dejection.

Confusion. (sometimes manifested by having difficulty concentrating, poor memory, or what is described as "painful thinking.") Depressed individuals often have difficulty in maintaining their patience with other people, especially loved ones, and they often have difficulty making decisions. This indecisiveness, decreased memory, and irritability form a triangle of disgust, wherein the depressed person becomes more and more disgusted with the unfulfilling nature of her lifestyle, and unfortunately those around her may become disgusted with her chronic problems. Depressed patients in this stage often lose their sense of humor and many times will withdraw from other people, preferring to be alone much of the time. There is often a tremendous internal sense of guilt or failure, and in fact, David understood the crushing nature of this despair when he said in Psalm 32:3: "When I kept silent about my sin, my body wasted away through my groaning all day long" (NASB).

Physical symptoms. Depression also may show itself initially through a variety of physical symptoms which may at first appear to be a medical illness.

- A pattern of poor sleep deteriorating into chronic insomnia
- Persistent fatigue
- Recurrent diarrhea or constipation without a detectable cause
- Loss of interest in a formerly enjoyable activity (especially a loss of sexual drive)
- Problems with memory or concentration
- Dizziness or unsteady gait
- Sudden changes in appetite or sudden weight gain or weight loss

Anxiety. A developing sense of tension and restlessness with no apparent cause that leads an individual to become less and less confident and to have less and less self-esteem may be one of the early signs of an oncoming depression. The sudden development of a phobia, especially agoraphobia, after age forty can almost always be linked to an underlying depression. Anxiety itself is an internal fear usually generated by either a dread of facing the truth about an internal part of one's personality such as a hidden motive or desire, or fear that comes from a long-repressed unconscious event in one's life.

Psychosis. The fifth symptom sometimes seen in depression is psychosis, or the loss of the ability to tell what is real from what is not real. Paranoia, delusions concerning one's own body configuration such as the irrational belief that one's internal organs are "rotting away," would be examples of the psychotic delusions of a severe depression. Sometimes auditory or visual hallucinations may occur and may even be interpreted as being "specific messages from God."

Causes of Depression

Depression can have any one of several causes. Although the actual sensation of depression is quite individual for each depressed person, the causes of depression can be grouped into four categories and can affect the restoration of the body.

1. Spiritual causes
2. Psychological causes
3. Situational causes
4. Physical causes

1) *Spiritual Cause of Depression:*
First, let us look at the unfortunate sequence of events which unfolds in the development of a depression brought on by a spiritual crisis, that is, unconfessed and persistent sin in the life of the believer.

SIN   The breaking of fellowship between God and man is the most devastating aspect of sin. Sin is a choice against God's biblical commands in pursuit of our own wants. The outcome of a willful refusal to obey God is that we will reap painful consequences (Hos. 8:7a).

ANXIETY   The Scriptures teach that sin not only causes a separation between God and man (Ps. 66:18), but sin causes anxiety in the heart of the believer. "I am full of anxiety because of my sin" (Ps. 38:18b, NASB).

      Confession and restoration of our relationship with the Lord can be one choice we make when we find ourselves under the anxiety caused by sin. "He who conceals his transgressions will not prosper, but he who confesses and forsakes them will find compassion" (Prov. 28:13, NASB).

DEPRESSION

Denial of the sin problem at hand, and a refusal to confess it and "make it right" with God now tumbles the Christian into real depression. Psalm 39:2 says that when we keep silent about our sin, the sorrow grows worse.

DESPAIR

Once depression is a continuous part of our existence, then the sadness of the heart can lead to brokenness (despair) of the very will to live (the spirit). "But when the heart is sad, the spirit is broken" (Prov. 15:13b).

"BREAKDOWN"

The final state of this process is a breakdown of the fabric of the personality, referred to in Scripture as a "drying up of the bones," and sometimes popularly known as a "nervous breakdown." "The spirit of a man can endure his (physical) sickness, but a broken spirit who can bear?" (Prov. 18:14, NASB).

2) *Psychological Causes of Depression:*

The psychological causes of depression would be those attitudes, priorities, and thought patterns which erode the healthy God-given self-esteem which Christians are supposed to have as children of the living God. The three most common psychological causes of depression are:

a. Anger turned inward
b. False guilt
c. Self-defeating prophecies

Anger turned inward usually results from rage and bitterness at personal injustices we feel we have suffered. When we feel too threatened to express anger, then it is often directed inwardly at some area of our own lives. The Christian who believes that it is always unacceptable to express anger will be at particular risk for developing a severe depression at sometime in her life due to the perpetual consequences of offense upon offense being accumulated and directed inwardly. The denial of this anger and its repression into other psychological defenses such as false humor, extreme obsessive and compulsive behavior, or rigid legalism of beliefs, is often a prelude to depression.

True guilt is that internal sense of having violated one's conscience in the face of an actual biblical standard. False guilt on the other hand is a chronic sense of having failed at achieving acceptance. False guilt may be precipitated by having internalized various social suggestions, taboos, or restrictions from parents and others during one's lifetime, and then finding it impossible to meet all of these imposed standards and guidelines. The two most likely groups of people to develop a depression because of overwhelming false guilt are the *workaholics* (individuals whose self-esteem is based on performance) and *applauseaholics* (those individuals who base their self-esteem on the ability to please others).

Possibly the most insidious and sometimes most prolonged psychological cause for depression is the self-defeating prophecy. A self-defeating prophecy is basically a wrong perspective on the inherent value of one's self to God. Such a sense of self-rejection is reinforced over the years by patterns of learned helplessness. Through the process of reinforcing failures, and then drawing conclusions as to one's own worthlessness, the self-defeating individual builds a house of hopelessness complete with all the comforts of despair.

3) *Situational Causes of Depression:*
Situational causes of depression have to do with personal setbacks that deal damaging blows to the stability of one's capacity to adjust to the circumstances of life. Such situational calamities usually fall into one of two categories: a) a loss of a tangible object,

b) a blow to the self-image. When an individual loses a spouse or a close friend, she suffers a very unsettling disruption of her life support system. Although the most common and certainly most devastating losses have to do with the loss of loved ones, losses of items such as one's job or one's health can certainly cause major disruptions within the personality. A major blow to the self-image is another situational factor which can predispose an individual to depression. When the Christian's self-image has become inadvertently based on anything other than her personal relationship with Jesus Christ, then she risks being severely shaken by a blow to her self-image. When an individual's self-image is severely shaken in a crisis, then she must ask herself whether her self-worth has been based on the accomplishments and identity of her own personhood, or has her self-worth truly been grounded in her identity before Jesus Christ? The Apostle Paul described his capacity to weather incredible assaults against his self-worth and self-image in 2 Corinthians 4:8–10,

> We are troubled on every side, yet not distressed; we are perplexed, but not in despair; persecuted, but not forsaken; cast down, but not destroyed; always bearing about in the body the dying of the Lord Jesus, that the life also of Jesus might be made manifest in our body.

No blow to our self-image can be truly shattering when our self-worth is so totally grounded in Jesus Christ.

4) *Physical Causes of Depression:*

A disruption in the physical processes of the mind can lead to the development of certain chemical imbalances within the nervous system causing depression. The list below outlines briefly fifteen different physical factors which can disrupt the natural processes of the mind enough to cause a depression.

1. An imbalance of neurotransmitters. The brain relies on several key chemical substances to maintain a stable level of mood at all times. For various genetic and medical reasons, some of which are not fully understood by medical science at this time, certain individuals can experience an imbalance in these vital neu-

rotransmitters. Such an imbalance can lead to major mood swings to depression and in some cases mania (the excessive elation and euphoric distortion of one's mood).

2. Hypoglycemia.

3. Hypothyroidism and/or hypoparathyroidism.

4. Endocrine hormone imbalances; for example, imbalances in blood levels of estrogen or adrenalin.

5. Imbalances in the minerals which circulate in the blood (electrolytes). Such electrolytes as sodium, potassium, and calcium are vital to the proper functioning of the brain.

6. Viral infections, such as the flu or infectious mononucleosis. Not only can depression accompany the acute phases of such illness, but also for several weeks thereafter in the recovery phase, the body seems particularly susceptible to depression.

7. Cancer of certain types, especially cancer of the pancreas, can be associated with lowering the mind's resistance to depression. This appears to be a separate process from the depression which can accompany a natural despondency from dealing with the fear of cancer itself.

8. The withdrawal from certain drugs such as amphetamines, cocaine, or high doses of marijuana can lead to depression.

9. Vitamin shortages or deficiencies, especially in the B-Complex vitamins and folic acid have been associated with the development of depression.

10. The use of certain drugs, especially alcohol and barbiturates, can imbalance the body toward the development of a depression.

11. The exposure to certain industrial poisons such as mercury, lead, arsenic, and bromide can precipitate a depression over a period of time.

12. Certain prescribed drugs can have the side effect of increasing the likelihood of depression. Medications such as propanolol, reserpine, and methyldopa that are used for the treatment of high blood pressure have been implicated in increasing the likelihood of depression. Also the prolonged use of steroids such as predinisone has been linked with depression in certain cases. Oral

contraceptives (birth control pills) should be considered as a possible cause of depression when the beginning of their use closely parallels the development of a depression in a young woman.

13. Certain chronic diseases of the joints and connective tissue in the body have been associated with diminishing the body's ability to resist depression, for example, lupus erythematosis, and polymyalgia rheumatica.

14. Pre-menstrual syndrome (PMS) has gained recognition lately as a potent causer of mood disruption. Apparently, the sudden alteration of hormones between ovulation and menstruation can lead to emotional destabilization in certain women. (For more information about PMS, see p. 76) Postpartum depressions which may occur in a woman after the birth of her baby have also been implicated as possibly having some basis in the major hormone shifts which occur in a woman's body after the termination of pregnancy through the delivery of a child.

15. Fatigue itself, especially fatigue over an extended period of time can significantly increase the risk of depression. God has designed the body to efficiently utilize the hours of sleep which we require to rebuild the stamina and clarity of our mental processes. Even the phenomenon of dreaming which accounts for about twenty minutes out of every ninety minutes that we sleep, plays a significant role in the maintenance of stable emotional functioning. Individuals who do not get enough sleep or who take drugs which decrease the amount of dreaming sleep can provoke the development of a depression.

These physical factors which can lead to the development of a depression must be diagnosed and treated by a qualified physician, preferably a psychiatrist who has speciality training in the proper care of physical disorders which can adversely affect the mind's function.

Dementia (senility)

Dementia is sometimes referred to as an Organic Brain Syndrome (OBS). It is a transient or permanent dysfunction of brain tissue caused by the brain cells either "wearing out" or being overcome by some toxin (such as alcohol or infection). The most common cause of dementia is loss of function due to senile aging; but other causes of dementia include chronic heart failure, multiple strokes, rapid changes in blood nutrients such as low protein, low thyroid hormone, toxic or poisonous substances in the blood such as alcohol or PCP, or even infections such as pneumonia or hepatitis. Another form of dementia which has gained much attention recently is Alzheimer's disease. This disorder is caused by a deterioration of the cells of the brain which are involved in recent memory, rational reasoning, good judgment, and control of impulsive behaviors.

Damage to the Brain

Damage to the intellectual apparatus of the mind can best be categorized as coming from either a) mental retardation, or b) brain injuries.

a. Mental retardation is defined as a below average general level of intellectual functioning, originating in childhood and associated with impairment of mature adaptive behavior.

b. Brain injuries. Any form of severe brain injury, for example, a concussion sustained in an automobile accident or the expanding pressure of a brain tumor can lead to mental changes. It appears that injuries to the frontal lobes (that area of the brain which rests directly behind the forehead) cause the most disruptive changes in personality.

Disintegration of Rational Thinking (schizophrenia)

Schizophrenia is possibly one of the most misunderstood of all mental illnesses. Unfortunately, the popular press has described the schizophrenic patient as having a "split personality." This is not really the case. Schizophrenics very rarely feel that they are two different people, and they do not have multiple personalities

with differing names for these personalities. In fact, the schizophrenic patient is acutely aware that he is present in this world. His
primary problem is an overwhelming inability to organize his
many thoughts and filter out what is real in his world from what is
unreal. Schizophrenia is the result of a chemical imbalance within the brain which appears to involve overactivation of brain cells
which utilize the brain neurochemical called dopamine. Although schizophrenia is not permanently curable, it is treatable
and can remain in remission with the use of proper medications,
very similar to the way in which diabetes is kept in remission
through the use of insulin.

Delusional Mania

Manic-depressive illness has certainly become one of the psychiatric diorders which is more widely known. Whereas
depression is manifested by withdrawal, despondency, and a general loss of energy, mania on the other hand is manifested by the
reverse. In effect the neurotransmitters in the brain which serve to
stab the emotions have become imbalanced and there develops an
explosive excess of emotional energy. This causes a decreased need
for sleep, rapid and illogical thinking, restlessness, excessive energy, and the loss of normal behavioral inhibitions.

Psychiatric disorders such as those mentioned in this chapter are
now well-recognized as medical conditions requiring treatment by
a doctor trained in the specialty of psychiatry. Unfortunately, in
the past, many Christians have fallen prey to obscure and un-
ethical treatments because of misinformation. If you feel that you
or someone you know needs treatment for a psychological condition, the care of a licensed psychiatrist should be sought.

Female Hormones and Your Emotions

There has recently been a tremendous interest in three syn-
dromes which are directly caused by hormone changes in the

female body. These are: premenstrual syndrome (PMS), menstrual distress syndrome (MDS), and menopause.

1. *Premenstrual syndrome (PMS)*: PMS is a psychophysiological disorder (it affects both the psychological and physical well-being of the sufferer). PMS may affect as many as one third of the women in the population to some degree, while approximately eight to ten percent will be severe enough to require treatment. PMS may begin spontaneously, or it may develop after the use of the pill, after a pregnancy, or sometimes after a major life stress. Although the exact cause of PMS is not known at this time, a disturbance of the estrogen-progesterone balance is suspected as the major causitive factor. The symptoms of PMS can include emotional tension and anxiety, headaches, backaches, swelling in the abdomen or breasts, craving for salty or sweet foods, digestion problems (diarrhea or constipation), acne eruptions, fatigue, excessively short temper, and/or depressed mood. Since this range of symptoms is quite wide, the diagnosis of PMS depends not only on the woman's having several of these symptoms, but also on the timing of the occurrence of her symptoms each month.

Usually the woman is relatively free of any such symptoms except for certain periods of the month, then she will suddenly and inexplicably develop some combination of these symptoms. Her discomfort is often great, and after the symptoms have run their course they frequently go away as quickly as they came. Others may not understand her condition, especially if the woman herself cannot explain it.

Although each woman's symptoms may vary, here are three symptom patterns commonly seen in PMS sufferers:

Pattern 1: *"Long Peakers"* These women have symptoms which begin around the twelfth to fourteenth day after the end of their previous menstrual period. (This is usually about the time of ovulation.) This woman's symptoms will usually worsen toward the twenty-eighth day of her cycle, and then relieve markedly with the beginning of her menstrual flow.

Pattern 2: *"Short Peakers"* These women have symptoms which may be every bit as severe as the "Long Peakers," but their symp-

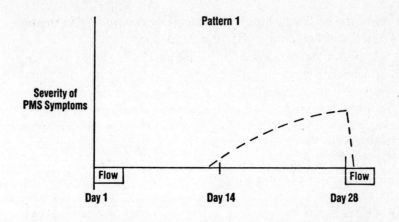

toms don't develop until about seven days before the twenty-eighth day of their monthly cycle. Their symptoms likewise relieve markedly with the beginning of menstrual flow.

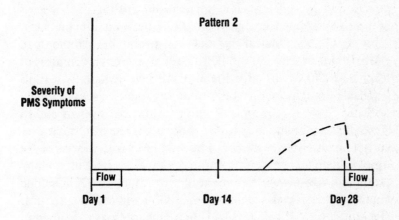

Pattern 3: *"Double Peakers"* These women are a little more difficult to diagnose because they experience PMS symptoms at two different points during their monthly cycle. Often they experience symptoms first on about the fourteenth day of their monthly cycle, generally around the time of ovulation. These symptoms diminish within two to three days, only to return again about five days prior to the beginning of menstrual flow. As in the other PMS

patterns, the beginning of menstrual flow usually brings a marked relief in symptoms.

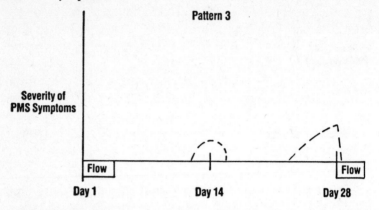

Uncontrolled PMS can significantly disrupt a woman's adjustment to life by diminishing her ability to cope with stress and eroding her self-esteem. The approach to treating PMS begins with a thorough gynecologic evaluation from a qualified medical specialist. Other physical disorders can mimic the symptoms of PMS, and thus they should be ruled out before the diagnosis of PMS is reached. Currently, the most effective treatment for PMS has been through the use of natural progesterone suppositories, prescribed during the time of month when the woman's PMS symptoms most frequently occur. Recently some encouraging results have also been achieved in treating PMS with the use of the drug Spironolactone, a drug commonly used to treat high blood pressure. Other general treatment considerations for PMS include taking adequate levels of vitamin B6 and B-complex, magnesium, and calcium. It is best to avoid stimulants such as caffeine and chocolate as well as depressants such as alcohol during PMS symptoms. Individual counseling, family counseling, and marital counseling are also often helpful in decreasing the amount of stress which PMS is bringing into the sufferer's personal life. When the proper diagnosis is made, PMS should be treated, not ignored. It will usually not go away on its own, and partial hysterectomy, tubal ligation, pregnancy, and aging rarely improve the course of PMS symptoms.

2. *Menstrual distress syndrome (MDS):* Menstrual distress syndrome has been known by a variety of different names through the years such as pre-menstrual tension, monthly "cramps," and backaches. MDS refers to that particular group of symptoms which may precede and last throughout the menstrual period. These symptoms may include abdominal bloating and cramping, anxiety, swelling in hands and feet, and irritability. In contrast to PMS, in MDS the woman's symptoms increase in severity during the menstrual flow and show a marked improvement at the end of menstrual flow. Treatment for MDS is generally directed toward the specific symptom which is causing the most difficulty. For example, excessive retention of fluid is often treated successfully with a decreased salt intake and use of a diuretic. Abdominal cramping, pelvic pain, and backache are often relieved successfully with medications such as Naproxen, Ibuprofen, Mefenamic Acid, or Indomethacin. These medications are frequently prescribed by gynecologists for this purpose. Concerning the psychological symptoms of MDS (irritability, nervousness, shakiness, and transient depression), the use of medications such as ergotamines, for example, Bellergal (trademark), can be useful as well as the occasional use of anti-anxiety medications such as Alprazolam. As always, the use of these medications requires the skilled evaluation and prescription by a qualified physician.

3. *Menopause:* Natural menopause results from the age-linked decline of function of the ovaries, which usually occurs between the ages of forty and fifty. The ovaries decrease in function and cease producing the levels of female hormones which they did previously during the years of regular menstrual cycles. The primary physical symptoms of menopause include occasional hot flashes and sweating due to vasomotor instability (the rapid changing of patterns of perspiration and blood circulation in the skin). Occasional back pain and joint weakness may also occur due to the osteoporosis (thinning of the bones) which can occur due to the decrease in circulating estrogen hormone after menopause. Many women are also concerned about the psychological symptoms which sometimes accompany menopause. These include fatigue, apathy, irritability, insomnia, heart palpatations, and even depres-

sion. If the psychological symptoms are severe, then a thorough evaluation by a qualified psychiatrist is necessary to rule out the possibility of an underlying depression. Fortunately, the emotional changes sometimes associated with menopause are often treatable with excellent results. Menopause should not be perceived in any way as a loss of ability or fulfillment for the Christian woman. It is God's natural physical change, designed by Him to set a limit on the length of child-bearing years. Although some specialized medical assistance may be needed to negotiate this change smoothly, the postmenopausal years for the Christian woman are very often her most productive years of contribution to the lives of her family, her church, and her community.

Study Questions

1. Have you ever experienced a depression that lasted for more than a day or two? Discuss.
2. Do you think you know the reason for that depression?
3. Dr. Byrd gives four causes of depression; discuss these remembering any cases.
4. What would be the first thing you would do when counseling someone who is depressed?
5. Do you experience the symptoms of premenstrual syndrome on a regular basis? If so, are you willing to see a gynecologist to check it out?

PART II

The Soul

Chapter 7
Introduction to the Soul

What's That in Your Vessel, Mud or Honey?

Our return from Myrtle Beach last August was sweetened considerably by a jar of honey that tipped over due to the pressure of the crowded back seat. It was a mess, but a sweet one, and Matt enjoyed tasting the sticky goo.

When something breaks, whether it be a valuable Ming vase or a Mason jar of honey, it is never pleasant, but it does happen. Whatever you have been filling your life with when the pressure, an accident, or carelessness tips, cracks, or squeezes you, will be what comes out. If you are a vase filled with the dirt of humanism and worldliness, when you are toppled by a crisis, the tears will mix with the dirt and muddy emotions will run out. Paul said (my paraphrase) "I was crushed . . . so much so that I despaired even of life, but that was to make me rely not on myself, but on the God who raises the dead" (2 Cor. 1:8, 9).

Last winter a chilling call came on a Sunday afternoon, just in time to hang a grey pall over Christmas. Lynn, age twenty-one, had been found dead in a forest with a self-inflicted bullet wound in her chest. It was especially painful for me because she was the daughter of my best friend, and I hadn't been able to help her. This young woman was a Christian who confided in me that she had attempted suicide before. She knew the Scriptures, and if anything, was worried that she was not spiritual enough. She had a young, healthy, and beautiful body that wasn't physically ill, but she had such deep-rooted emotional problems which she could not come to grips with that she finally broke. She talked with me about spiritual things and about aerobics as a treatment for depression, but she never honestly revealed her emotional hurts to me. I wondered what more I could have done to prevent that young life from being cut down like a sapling in the forest.

Last week I answered the phone to hear a hysterical young woman crying—practically screaming about how hurt she was. Her relatively new husband had already been unfaithful. This dynamic young Christian was crying out, "Why did this happen to me? I just wish I were dead." Later, while holding the crushed young woman, we discussed alternatives to death and how the Lord loved her and would forgive *through* her if she allowed Him. In a few hours she pulled her head up, agreed to forgive her husband, and went home saying, "Satan has tried to win a victory, but the Lord can use this for good."

What was the difference between the young woman who did commit suicide and the next young woman who was pressured to that point? The woman who was only pressured to the point of suicide dealt with her emotions right up front. Loudly, tearfully. She was able to separate the spiritual from the emotional. She felt horrible, her world had crashed, but that didn't mean she had lost God's love or that she deserved punishment. Her husband felt badly too. He didn't realize how unprepared he was for temptation. He gave in to a harmful emotion, lust, and that set the stage for this painful scene. She didn't feel unspiritual coming for help. It is a rare Christian indeed who recognizes that God *understands* when they need to cry out in their pain.

One young woman was afraid to explore the emotional depths,

and rather than face whatever it was, she departed. That young woman is dead; the other is living. Still vulnerable, guaranteed to be hurt again and again in this life, but living.

There is yet another woman I know who, under pressure from five children, no money, and many sorrows, just walked away from her family and started a new life without them.

There are countless women who haven't run away or killed themselves, but have wanted to do both. They pride themselves that they are stronger, so they layer one emotional disappointment, injury, or anger upon the last one, until their vessel is so filled with harmful emotions that even if they don't blow, their whole being is poisoned. The poison from that stoic spills over into the lives of those they touch, and they in turn carry over into their lives the same harmful emotions. Our mental hospitals and prisons are filled with those who never learned how to deal with their emotions. Whole families are buried together because someone flew into a rage that had been ignited much earlier. Some fuses burn slowly, while others reach the explosive stage immediately. How about you?

What are we to do with our emotions? Are they evil in their own right? No, we are created in the image of God, and deeply imprinted on that image is a network of emotions that, if properly managed, can be enjoyed.

In seeking to become a balanced woman, I found I was one of many who handle their emotions incorrectly. Many women are either *run by* their emotions with no control over them, or they overcontrol them. They build walls or bury emotions rather than learn to deal with them honestly. We see the results in battered children, alcoholic and drug-dependent women, as well as in an epidemic number of suicides.

Dr. James Dobson says the following in *Emotions—Can You Trust Them?*

Emotions must always be accountable to the faculties of reason and will. That accountability is doubly important for those of us who purport to be Christians. If we are to be defeated during life's spiritual pilgrimage, it is likely that negative emotions will play a dominant role in that discouragement. Satan is devastatingly effective in using the weapons of guilt, rejection, fear, embarrassment, grief, depression, loneliness and misunderstanding.

Someone wrote, "The mind, body, and soul are very close neighbors, and one usually catches the ills of the others."

The soul is the seat of our emotions, and because of that, it is the most colorful part of our being. In it lie our temperament, personality, abilities, and feelings. The care of the soul is as important as care of the body, so let's take a look at the proper cleansing, diet, exercise, clothing, and restoring of it.

Study Questions

1. Can you remember a time you were pressured to the point of wanting to give up? Are you willing to share this with the group?
2. Do you think it is wrong to express your deepest feelings with one who cares or should you keep them inside?
3. What happens to people who continuously bury their feelings?
4. Do you agree with Dr. James Dobson that "emotions must always be accountable to the faculties of reason and will"?
5. Name some negative emotions Satan uses to discourage Christians.

Chapter 8
Cleansing the Soul

What Happened and How Did You Feel?

September 1975 found me picking up the pieces after a suicide attempt. The move from Gadsden, Alabama to Tampa, Florida was very painful. The fact that I could keep my secret swept under the proverbial rug in a new place was the only asset.

Soon after arriving in the area I met a vivacious, blonde woman who appeared to have it all together. I so admired her that I asked her to be my prayer partner. She said, "I would love to, but we would have to pray at the office."

"That's fine with me, where is it?"

She wrote down the address on a card of a crisis center I passed nearly every day and told me that she and her husband managed it. I felt like running but decided I could pray in the crisis center without ever letting on that I had a crisis of my own. Wrong! After two weeks I told the lovely, joyful blonde that my life was anything but joyful and that I was depressed. She advised me to see one of the psychologists but I said, "You don't seem to understand. We are in a ministry, and if anyone found out I was going for counseling it would be terrible."

"Don't be silly! Everyone could benefit from some counseling now and then. I have."

I made an appointment, and what I feared was true: I began to see myself as never before. It was during one such appointment that the psychologist was trying to help me separate my body, soul, and spirit so that I could determine whether my problems were physical, emotional, or spiritual. I'm sure she knew all three were involved. She would then show me how to integrate them in a healthy way. But, I found that I had a form of amnesia. When asked about my relationship with my husband I became defensive. "Oh, no you don't, you can't blame him." I began explaining how wonderful my husband was. I told her how often I wished for a sanguine, happy disposition like his. I explained how patient and caring he had always been. I went on extolling his virtues, of which he has many.

The psychologist said, "You have said enough that I think there is a problem here." Wisely sensing my "quick-freeze," she changed the subject to one showing me how to find out about myself in the privacy of my own home. She gave me the chart on the next page to keep in this exploration.

Emotional Inventory Chart

WHAT HAPPENED?	HOW I FELT?	WHAT I DID?	WHAT WAS THE RESULT?

I left the session disturbed. I didn't know then that the status quo often has to be disturbed in order for healing to begin. Gangrenous flesh must be cut away so healthy flesh can grow. I was to begin removing the scab from my infected soul, but I didn't even know it.

Something else disturbed me. I didn't think anything in my life was significant enough to write down on a dumb chart! I didn't even really know why I was depressed.

As I climbed into my car the temperature probably registered 110 degrees, even though I was parked under a skimpy tree. It was September; it was the humid heat of Florida, and I was beginning to think honestly. "I wish I had had this chart before our move in June. I would have written under the WHAT HAPPENED? column: My husband accepted a job offer and move when I was too ill and fatigued with life even to consider it. WHAT HAPPENED? I was so depressed and unable to cope that the move was the straw that broke the camel's back and I tried to bow out. WHAT HAP- PENED? We moved anyway! I clenched my teeth and hands as I looked at the column headed, HOW I FELT? Momentarily I didn't squash what I felt, and I knew what I would have written, ANGRY!

I also felt anger as we drove up the brown, sandy drive to face a house that was extremely hard for me to deal with. Knowing now that my frame of mind made the house uglier than it really was didn't help the anger that I still felt. Maybe the psychologist had a point. Marvin's extreme optimism made this house look good to him, but he wasn't being very sensitive to me. Enough thinking those thoughts; that is not very Christian. So I buried them and claimed amnesia again. It was more comfortable than finding a way to deal with the anger.

It was time for three children to come home. Getting out cookies and pouring glasses of milk, I wondered if I should *make up* something to put on the chart. Nothing big seemed to happen.

I took my guard position in the kitchen when I heard them coming, arguing as usual. As they pushed each other through the door, I noticed the knees of Matt's jeans were out again. Mark threw his dirty gym clothes down by the washer. Twelve-year-old

"Puberty Polly," Mandi was crying about how she hated the new school, and then they all began to talk to me at once. A glass of milk was spilled on cue. It happened every day. I began to yell until they quieted. Every day I waited for them to come in and tell me what a neat mom they had and how they loved me. I hoped one day they would come home clean and orderly and loving each other, but it never happened. I felt horrible.

In tears I ran to the bedroom. As I lay across the four-poster bed where those same children had been conceived, I pulled the folded chart from under my purse, and I began to write:

WHAT HAPPENED?	HOW I FELT?	WHAT I DID?	WHAT WAS THE RESULT?
Kids came home	Angry	Yelled	Guilt

Boy! Did that look stupid in writing. Oh, well, I just wouldn't go back to the counselor. I decided to keep the chart for my own information.

About an hour later I dragged my weary body into the kitchen to prepare dinner. After finally getting through another meal with the usual teasing, fussing, and messing, I began another nightly ritual. I was trying to teach Mandi how to clean the kitchen, and it seemed she delighted in spilling things and rubbing grease around. During the squabbling, I was also trying to teach six-year-old Matt three verses for his school assignment. He was bright but couldn't seem to memorize. Before we realized that he had a learning disability I felt as if he was pushing me back and forth on an emotional seesaw. Where was my delightful, fun-loving husband? Keeping HIS sanity in the bedroom. Every night he sat at his desk, studied his Bible, and listened to Christian music.

I knew I could never go back for counseling after I wrote, "My husband is in the bedroom listening to music and reading his Bible while the kitchen is quickly becoming a disaster area." HOW DID I FEEL ABOUT IT? ANGRY!

The next week, I did go back, with a chart filled with "little" irritations that were adding up to one big emotion—*Anger*. When I settled down on the brown leather sofa, the lid was off, the amnesia was gone, and I was spilling over. The doctor smiled. She was not disappointed in my Christianity but pleased that I allowed myself to look into me, and I began to admit what I felt. She explained that once I saw it and admitted it I could be helped.

"You know, it's not big things, but everyday little annoyances that are driving me to the cookie factory."

"Yes," she said, "but those little things are like little shoots on a plant that make a big root, and once it is allowed to stay and be watered and fed, it is a big thing. We must get at the root of it."

"How?" I asked.

"First, you must confess your anger towards your husband, children, the house. Then you must realize and confess that you even have anger towards God."

"You're right, because God is God and He could make things easier or better but He doesn't always do it," I replied.

"It is good that you recognize that. Once you confess your anger towards God, you will be cleansed, but in order to have a clean soul and healthy emotions, you must forgive them. Forgive your husband for the moves, your children for fighting like normal kids, and then learn how to deal with the angry feelings when they come, for they will come."

1 John 1:9 says, "If we confess our sins, he is faithful and just to forgive us our sins, and to cleanse us from all unrighteousness."

With all the horrible years of angers finally brought out into the open and confessed, I knew God's Word is true and I was forgiven. On to step two. I decided to choose to forgive all the past hurts that I could remember. But how to keep the build-up from beginning again? The psychologist asked me a few questions and I will just use two that refer to the illustrations of anger I have given. "Can you:

1. When it is time for your children to come home from school, leave the cookies and milk on the counter and go into another room?"

"Who me, Mary Martyr?" Didn't I have to be there to take my

licks and see them just in case they would one day come in looking as if they hadn't been at school all day, playing on dusty playgrounds and getting their clothing torn?

Understanding that I had set my goals too high, I tried it the next day. By the time they found me in another room ironing, they came in one at a time. I didn't see the overwhelming evidence that life was the same that week as it had been the week before. Sure, they spilled milk, but I didn't know it until the next day when my feet stuck to the floor, and by then I could handle it without feeling angry.

I have now progressed to the point that if I don't put cookies and milk out, I know I'm not a failure as a mother. I have taken myself out of the box I built, labeled "Good Mother," that had no flexibility. Now I can enjoy the children, and as some have grown and left home, they tell me I am the best mother in the world. Now my goals are more attainable, and everyone is more comfortable.

2. "Have you ever explained to your husband your view of the after-dinner scene and even told him you resent it?"

Not Mary Martyr! This is a woman who baked herself a Mother's Day cake when she had two little kids, was about to deliver another, and no one remembered "her" day. Could I do it?

That evening I stiffly walked to the bedroom and forced myself to say through clenched teeth: "Marvin, I resent this."

"Resent what?"

I didn't dare say I resented him reading his Bible or listening to Christian music, so I worded it to say that it was his timing and withdrawal from family development.

I nearly collapsed when he said three very important words to a mother, "Can I help?" He took over the job of memorization.

The verse 1 Peter 1:6 that talks about the heaviness through manifold trials says it is "for a season." That means those problems were temporary, they are gone now, replaced by new "temporary trials."

From that time on I have tried to deal honestly with how I feel and keep short accounts. I don't go for hitting pillows or the walls or screaming abuse at someone. We may have gone too far in some respects getting people to express their anger. Again we need a happy balance.

When I understood the following verse, I realized that forgiveness extended toward others is the soap and water I needed to bathe my soul every day:

> For if you forgive people their trespasses—that is, their reckless and willful sins, leaving them, letting them go and giving up resentment—your heavenly Father will also forgive you. But if you do not forgive others . . . neither will your Father forgive you your trespasses (Matt. 6:14–15, AMPLIFIED).

The more I became free to discover my inner self, the more poison I saw—poisons that not only made families ill, but spread throughout homes, relationships, churches, schools, communities, and the world. Wars are going on everywhere. I saw that while our network of emotions are good, if not handled correctly, they can become killers. Vitamins, while good for you, can be deadly if overdosed. Two aspirins can relieve a headache and that is good, but a whole bottle can kill. Now, let's examine the matter of stress, how detrimental it is, and how to cleanse it from our soul.

Stress Kills

The matter of stress is one which concerns all of us, for we all live under a certain amount of stress. When I was doing my medical training at the University of Texas Medical School in San Antonio, there was an interesting sign which one of the surgeons had placed above the door to the operating suite dressing room. The sign read "Stress Kills," and it had been put there by one of the surgeons to remind those of us in training that indeed the amount of pressure which we carried internally would have a direct bearing on the longevity of our lives. A recent major medical article reported several studies which added a fourth name to the previous big three risk factors for heart attacks. The so-called "big three" risk factors which had been recognized for a long time as greatly increasing one's chances for a heart attack were cigarette smoking, high blood pressure, and elevated blood cholesterol. The fourth factor which has now earned an equal rating in the increasing of heart attack risk is stress. Stress (or the inner sense of pressure and tension) is now recognized as a major factor in increasing the risk of heart disease. Those individuals who are most stress prone are referred to in medical literature as having Type A personalities. The three main behavioral characteristics of Type A personalities are:

1. They have a hard-driving temperament. Type A personalities often place themselves under self-imposed standards that are unrealistically ambitious and which they pursue in an inflexible fashion. Associated with this is a need to maintain productivity in order to be respected and they may even show a sense of guilt while on vacation or taking time to personally relax. They may appear to those around to be possessed by an unrelenting urge for recognition or power. They seem to always maintain a competitive attitude in everything they do. Increased muscular activity in the form of gestures or motions or facial activities such as grimaces, gritting and grinding of teeth, or tensing of the jaw muscles is common. Pounding of the fist to make a point, fidgeting or tapping feet or even playing with a pencil in rhythmic fashion are favorites of the Type A personality.

2. Type A personalities maintain a high level of job involvement and often manifest persistence, vigilance, and a keen anticipation of circumstances in their job setting. When unpredicted events occur, they often react impulsively and quickly. They seem to be able to follow several lines of action and several trains of thought simultaneously.

3. Speed and impatience are two qualities which hallmark the Type A personality. Their quick responsiveness and impatience may be manifested by a tendency to interrupt or finish in another person's response in conversation. Their conversation is marked by varying speech volume and pitch and they may alternate rapid

bursts of speech with long pauses or even deep sighing breaths for emphasis. They are often self-centered and tend to be poor listeners. Many times they have an air of some degree of superiority or at least give the impression of being too busy to be bothered by very much unproductive conversation. They are prone to push others as hard as they push themselves in the pursuit of the priorities which they have set for themselves, their jobs, and even their families.

If we see stress as the result of pressures from the outside causing tension on the inside of our personalities, then what are the most common causes of stress in the life of the Christian? The following are five different factors which can cause undue stress in the life of the believer.

Factor 1. Unscriptural goals or unwise priorities. The Christian who is pursuing a lifestyle which is in conflict with God's order of priorities and God's promises within Scripture is inevitably going to find herself under a tremendous amount of stress. Isaiah 57:20–21. Living outside God's will for the Christian is the epitome of living in stress.

Factor 2. Unreasonable people. Not only does God warn the Christian woman in Proverbs 21:19 not to become a source of stress to others, but it is also unwise for her to become influenced by the actions of unreasonable or untrustworthy individuals.

Factor 3. Being unyielded to the Lord in an area where His will has been made clear. Such a decision to become stubborn or stiff-necked in resisting the intentions of the Lord can lead to personal calamity and a tremendous amount of stress therein. See Proverbs 29:1.

Factor 4. Unpredictable events which cause a sudden change in the status quo of our lives. The following table shows a list of events which can have a significant and often sudden impact on our lives. Many of them are negative but many of them are not, the common denominator being that they all serve to cause significant change in one's life. The larger the impact of the change, the greater the stress which that change may bring. The two researchers, Homes and Rahe, found that an accumulation of 200 or more life change units in a single year causes enough stress to be followed by a significant increase in psychiatric disorders.

The Stress of Adjusting to Change

Events	Scale of Impact
Death of a spouse	100
Divorce	73
Marital separation	65
Jail term	63
Death of a close family member	63
Personal injury or illness	53
Marriage	50
Fired at work	47
Marital reconciliation	45
Retirement	45
Change in health of family member	44
Pregnancy	40
Sex difficulties	39
Gain of new family member	39
Business readjustment	39
Change in financial state	38
Death of close friend	37
Change to different line of work	36
Change in number of arguments with spouse	35
Mortgage over $10,000	31
Foreclosure of mortgage or loan	30
Change in responsibilities at work	29
Son or daughter leaving home	29
Trouble with in-laws	29
Outstanding personal achievement	28
Spouse begins or stops work	26
Begin or end school	26
Change in living conditions	25
Revision of personal habits	24

Although an individual may undergo a significant amount of
stress in a given period of time, unlike the non-Christian, the
Christian has a refuge to turn to in the most difficult of times.
Christ Himself stated the case eloquently in Matthew 11:28,
NASB.

Come to Me, all who are weary and heavy-laden, and I will give you
rest. Take My yoke upon you, and learn from Me, for I am gentle and
humble in heart; and you shall find rest for your souls. For My yoke is
easy, and My load is light.

Factor 5. Actions or words of unrestrained anger. The chronic
presence of anger in the heart of a Christian, coupled with impulsive or unthinking actions, can produce a tremendous amount
of stress over a period of time. There are generally two types of
anger: "healthy" anger which is anger toward a sin and not toward
a person; and "unhealthy" anger which is directed toward a person, and it always causes stress. In the following chapter we will
discuss in detail how to handle anger properly.

We've seen how stress can be a true destroyer of our emotional
fabric. When you sense that you are under undue stress or tension,

here are seven "T's" which you may want to use as a checklist in decreasing the amount of stress which you are placing yourself under.

1. *Tell the Lord all the details of the situation and trust Him fully for a word of comfort and direction.* 1 Peter 5:7 tells us to cast all our anxiety upon Him because He cares for us, and Isaiah 41:10 (NASB) says, "'Do not fear, for I am with you; do not anxiously look about you, for I am your God. I will strengthen you, surely I will help you, surely I will uphold you with My righteous right hand.'"

2. *Become threshold conscious.* Learn to take a break when you need a change of pace. No matter how short a period of time it may be, a small break may serve to "defuse" a situation and give you a new outlook on an old problem.

3. *Teach yourself to relax.* Learning to relax is not something that comes naturally for a lot of Christians. We have to teach ourselves to take time to recharge our batteries and unscramble our thoughts. Just a few minutes of peace and quiet every day can make a big difference.

4. *Take exercising seriously.* Regular exercise not only strengthens your body and thereby improves your body's ability to function smoothly under pressure, but also serves to provide a physical outlet for many of the everyday frustrations we all experience.

5. *Time, plan, and prioritize your work.* Tension and anxiety can really build up when your work seems endless. Plan your work to use time and energy as efficiently as possible, and seek to get those jobs out of the way first which are the most likely to produce stress if they are left uncompleted.

6. *Don't be theoretical; be realistic.* People who expect too much of themselves get tense if things don't work out. Set very practical goals and expect to be successful at taking care of the jobs which you have set before yourself in "bite size" portions. Even the most overwhelming of tasks can usually be solved by accomplishing small goals on a daily basis.

7. *Terminate certain activities and involvements.* Learn to say "no" diplomatically but firmly. God intends for each of His chil-

dren to run the race which He has set before them. The stagnant and lazy Christian who refuses to run the race to which God has called him certainly is an unfortunate sight, but equally tragic is the Christian who has been called to run a race, but illadvisably "burns himself out" in the first half mile by failing to eliminate some of the good involvements in life in order to selectively include the very best involvements.

Study Questions

1. Would you agree to counseling if you had a problem that you couldn't seem to resolve? Or do you think it is shameful for a Christian to seek counseling?
2. Use the enclosed chart for a week, writing down even the smallest things that disturb you. Next week discuss with the group.
3. After reading Matthew 6:14–15, what would you say is the cleansing for the soul?
4. What are the three main behavioral characteristics of the most stress-prone individuals?
5. Name five factors which can cause undue stress in the life of the believer.
6. Discuss the seven "T's" which will decrease the amount of stress you put yourself under.

Chapter 9
Feeding the Soul

Name Your Poison

People who tell you never to let little things bother you have never tried sleeping in a room with a mosquito.—Katherine Chandler

I wonder how many red-eyed people who belly up to their local bar understand the hidden truth in the bartender's phrase "Name your poison"? In the beginning, alcohol warms and gives temporary feelings of peace and well-being. But every year at graduation time, you can read of a young person finishing off a fifth of whiskey at one time and finishing off himself from alcohol poisoning.

Our emotions, properly managed, contribute to our well-being, but out of control, like alcohol, they become a destructive force and a family disease. Author David Ausburger says, "Conflict is neither good nor bad, right or wrong. Conflict simply is. How we view, approach, and work through our differences does—to a large extent—determine our whole life pattern."

Working through our conflicts calls for well-controlled emotions.

Harmful Soul Foods

Hostility comes from the Latin word *hostilis*, meaning "enemy." One dictionary says it is an "unfriendly attitude; antagonism, opposition, or resistance in thought or principle." But it is really a deadly, poisonous root shooting out tender sprouts that can wind themselves around the flowers of your life and strangle them. These shoots are:

 Poison 1—Anger: In the previous chapter, Dr. Byrd discussed what anger can do to a life. At first I was horrified to be labeled "angry." I didn't classify myself as an angry person. I don't have a hot temper, and I don't throw things. I found that, like bellybuttons, we are in two categories: the Insies and the Outsies. I'm an Insie. I can allow anger to stay within me, seething until I feel guilty about feeling angry; so then I turn the anger in on myself. This in turn leads to self-destructive thoughts: "I must really be no good to feel this way about my children. After all they are just children. They can't help tearing the knees out and getting dirty. Shame on me for feeling this way. I must be bad."

I have a good friend who is definitely an Outsie, and I can be sure she will verbally correct any unfair situation whether it be bad service in a restaurant or a snippy sales girl. Sometimes I get embarrassed at her displays of anger, but we are both dealing with anger in the wrong way.

What should we do about anger? Isn't anger always sinful? No, it's not. God Himself, Who is perfect righteousness and the essence of love, is also capable of anger. In the Old Testament, the word *anger* appears over 450 times, and 375 of those times relate to God's anger. Unhealthy anger, or unrighteous anger, is rooted in selfishness and a lack of belief in the genuine sovereignty of God for all situations. The following chart matches the basic root causes of unrighteous anger with the beliefs which give rise to them.

Roots of Anger:	Causes for Anger:
1. Greed (Prov. 28:25)	1. What I don't have
2. Jealousy (Prov. 6:34)	2. What others do or what happens to them
3. Hatred (Prov. 10:12)	3. Who or what other people are
4. Envy (Prov. 24:1, 19–20)	4. What others have (things)
5. Gossip (Prov. 18:8)	5. What others represent
6. Criticism (Mocker) (Prov. 22:10)	6. Poor self-concept so I have to put others down to make me feel exalted
7. Bottom Line = PRIDE (Prov. 13:10)	7. Angry at God for your position in life

There are generally three ways to handle anger:

1. *Express it.* This involves the releasing or "letting go" of one's angry emotions, sometimes in an explosive fashion. In the early days of psychotherapy, this was encouraged as a means of catharsis that would leave the personality cleaned out of angry or frustrated emotions. Some recent evidence has shown, however, that the simple expression of anger may do very little to decrease its overall presence or its internal stress. Like tears, which seem to come from an inexhaustible reservoir, anger in the heart of man seems to be present in an inexhaustible quantity if the only solution is to remove it by expressing it regularly.

2. *Repress it.* The repression or internal concealment of anger is a very dangerous psychological action to take. In fact, some of the most severe depressions and especially those which involve suicidal attempts are often connected with anger which has been "turned inward" through years of denial. The simple repressing of anger on a consistent basis has no real validity in the Christian's approach to the problem.

3. *Confess it.* In the Greek language the word for "confess" carries the literal meaning of "to come to an agreement with." When we are angry about a matter, and in fact, the matter has

caused us significant stress due to the lack of our ability to find an acceptable way to deal with our anger about it, it is only through the prayerful seeking of the mind of Christ that we find a way to truly resolve our angry feelings. Confessing our anger involves letting the Lord see every angry thought, every bitter attitude, and every impulsive action tangled up in the snarl of our rage. As we, piece by piece, take this tangled web of emotions apart in front of His watchful eye, and pray point by point for His perspective on each one of our attitudes, we see the genuine resolving and healing of anger and bitterness. David understood keenly the stress it caused when he refused to confess and resolve a matter between himself and the Lord (Ps. 32:3–5).

The first step in "confessing" anger is to realize that there are three types of anger:

1. Instant anger (reflex anger)
2. Daily anger
3. "Deep-rooted" anger

Instant Anger (reflex anger)

Instant anger is almost a reflex because of its rapid onset. It is that immediate rage which we feel when encountering the hassles, irritants, and tiny transgressions of life. It's the anger you feel when you're driving in your automobile and someone pulls out in front of you in a dangerous and inconsiderate way. It's the anger you feel when someone at work steals your favorite coffee cup or takes an inconsiderate action which will cost you valuable time. This kind of anger occurs almost before you realize it and the biblical response to this kind of anger is to willfully *overlook* it. In essence, this is looking beyond the offense at hand to the person of Jesus. You are raising your "spiritual eyes" above the relatively minor irritation that has occurred, and instead of focusing on the offense, you are focusing on the character and compassion of Jesus Christ. Proverbs 19:11 says that it is the mark of a wise man to overlook a transgression. This looking to the person of Jesus involves taking a moment to think of how He would respond in the situation, and also directing your mind to possibly retrieve from memory a verse of Scripture which may deal with the situation. Ephesians 5:26 states that our mind can be continually washed by the Word of God, and since Jesus is the living Word, the immediate shifting of our mental focus off the minor irritant which has provoked our anger and onto the written Word and finished work of Jesus Christ is how a mature Christian deals with instant anger.

Daily Anger

The second kind of anger is called daily anger because it involves anger which has built up through the course of a day. It accumulates in a slower fashion than the previously mentioned instant anger. In other words, it "simmers" throughout the day through the accumulation of offenses. The Scripture begins to give us guidelines for dealing with this daily anger in Ephesians 4:26–27. There we see that we may be angry but we are not to sin against God by letting the sun go down on our anger. Although the existence of this anger may not be sin, the failure to try to resolve it by the end of the day is sin. Not dealing with it properly by the end of the day gives the devil an opportunity to spiritually cripple us with an emotional thorn. The Scriptures tell us plainly in several passages how to deal with daily anger. Leviticus 19:17–18 (NASB) states,

> You shall not hate your fellow-countryman in your heart; you may surely reprove your neighbor, but shall not incur sin because of him. You shall not take vengeance (revenge) nor bear any grudge against the sons of your people, but you shall love your neighbor as yourself; I am the Lord.

The Scriptures are telling us here that revenge and hatred are not acceptable means of dealing with offenses which cause us to be angry. In Matthew 18:15–17, Christ gives the sequence we are to follow in resolving our differences with an offended brother or sister.

First, we are to go and "reprove" the person in private. This does not mean launching an assault on the individual's personal character or leveling an overall criticism of his or her lifestyle. It does mean in a precise, compassionate, and gentle manner we are to approach the individual and deal with the area of offense. If you resolve the matter at that level, then the Scripture says that you have won your brother. Resolving the matter at this level may involve:

Clarifying points of misunderstanding,
Compromising on nonessential differences,
Confession of personal wrongdoing,
Calling for mutual forgiveness for unthinking or inconsiderate actions.

Second, if a brother will not reach a point of resolution concerning an offense and anger therefore continues to be a problem, the Scriptures tell us in Matthew 18:16 that we are to call a "small conference" of two or three unbiased witnesses to hear the matter discussed openly and honestly. Unfortunately, this is rarely done within the church, but without this second step in dealing with angry matters of offense, the likelihood is that the anger involved will continue long after the sun goes down many times. Instead of resolving such matters in a healthy fashion, unfortunately Christians tend to gripe, gossip, or go inside with (repress) their anger. *Griping* causes a breakdown in our relationship with God; *gossipping* causes a breakdown in our relationship with other people; and *going inside* (repressing internally) causes a breakdown of our physical bodies through stress.

Third, if the offense continues and the anger will not be settled, then the final step within the church is to go before the pastor and elders (spiritually mature leadership) of the church and ask them for a ruling. The Scriptures say that they have the power to separate a brother or sister from the fellowship over the matter of chronically unresolved anger and bitterness. This may seem like harsh action, but the alternative is to allow the emotional cancer of bitterness to spread.

Deep-Rooted Anger

The third kind of anger is deep-rooted anger. This anger is not an anger which can be attributed to an event in the immediate past. Instead, this deep-rooted anger is a chronic, smoldering kind of rage which has been around long enough to develop into bitterness. The Scriptures tell us in Hebrews 12:15 that we must not allow any root of bitterness to exist within our lives, for it will surely defile the entire quality of our Christian life. There are countless thousands of Christians whose lives have been defiled (rendered spiritually ineffective) by the continual presence of bitterness and resentment within their hearts. Again, the Scriptures give us a process by which we can remove a root of bitterness from our heart.

First, we are to confess this bitterness to God as sin. Regardless of the severity of the event in question, and regardless of the cruelty of the person(s) responsible for it, God never approves of bitterness. It is the vilest form of spiritual poison, and the first step in ridding our soul of it is to confess it as sin. 1 John 1:9 says:

> If we confess our sins, he is faithful and just to forgive us our sins, and to cleanse us from all unrighteousness.

Second, we must bind the devil. This is simply maintaining the practice of regular prayer that God will restrain Satan from defeating, discouraging, or distracting us as we go about the process of reconciliation. Bitterness in the heart of a Christian can become the domain of Satan because of his longstanding stronghold there. Hence, as we approach the process of reconciling this bitterness we must bind Satan from interfering. Matthew 12:29 says that before the domain of a strong man can be entered, he must be bound securely. Binding Satan is simply calling on the Lord through the power of the Holy Spirit to restrain him from working his mischief as we go about the process of restoring a right relationship with God through the resolution of chronic inner bitterness (see 1 John 4:4).

Third, we should ideally go to the person and ask his or her forgiveness for our longstanding bitter attitude. You may not be forgiven and in fact you may be shunned or ridiculed, but God sees the intent of your heart.

Please note: It is not always wise to go to a person toward whom you have had an inner and private aversion and make an open disclosure of it. In such cases your personal resolution of the matter before the Lord may be best. We suggest that you procure wise spiritual counsel from your pastor or other spiritually mature person when dealing with this kind of a situation.

In general, we should do what we can to rectify any wrong. In James 2:15–18 we are told that faith (having a heart full of good intentions) is only half the process of obedience. Faith must be followed by works with the purpose of honoring the Lord Jesus Christ. For example, if the offense occurred as a result of an unsettled debt, then write a check and pay the debt. If the offense was due to a story told in gossip, then try to find the parties who were misled and replace the gossip with truth. Even if a true story were told which resulted in the damaging of someone's character, then after apologizing to the injured person, go to those individuals with whom you shared this information and apologize to them for wrongfully allowing yourself to speak ill of someone (see Romans 14:4).

Fourth, we must realize that there are some individuals who will never reciprocate our desire to resolve a longstanding offense. There were those who hated Christ right up to the day of His crucifixion, and yet He was at peace with them because there was no bitterness or hatred in His heart. Luke 6:27–28 states,

> But I say unto you which hear, Love your enemies, do good to them which hate you, bless them that curse you, pray for them which despitefully use you.

Your conscience will be clear, your relationship with God will be restored, and your effectiveness for the cause of Christ will abound when you have reached the point of forgiving and forgetting offenses that have caused a bitter spirit to reside in your heart. Once you have expended all the means available to you to reconcile an issue between yourself and another individual, then God excuses you from the task and you are free from the bondage of these past events.

 Poison 2—Greed and Jealousy, by "Old Green Eyes": Who hasn't felt the stirrings of jealousy? Old Covet Face reminds you that Sara Slim eats twice as much as you and wears a size five. How many diets have been started out of jealousy? You find yourself asking—is it worth it and is it fair?

Phthonos is the Greek word that is translated "envy" in the New Testament and denotes a strong displeasure over the advantages of others' prosperity.

It is difficult to remember Paul's saying, "For I have learned, in whatsoever state I am, therewith to be content" (Phil. 4:11). You cringe, knowing the Lord would have you to pray for blessings on those who don't have to struggle for every dime like you.

I believe lust, greed, and jealousy all stem from the loss of contentment. The dictionary says being content is "happy enough with what one has or is; not desiring something more or different; satisfied." Dissatisfaction is a national disease. Wanting to better ourselves is not wrong, but at what point are we satisfied? For awhile after my decision to receive Christ, I found complete satisfaction in Him. I didn't care for material things and for a time was not bothered with jealousy. I mistakenly thought that was a new way of life. But it wasn't long until I found myself jealous over who got to sing in church or who was a better teacher than myself. Well, the ugly old sin was still around to be indulged in. I found I had to make a choice—indulge or resist. Old habits had to be broken. Sometimes it is hard to spot greed and jealousy in another, but that is not our job. It is our duty to spot it in ourselves, judge it, and check it

Philippians 2:3–4 and Psalm 37:4–5 show us how the poison of envy can be eliminated:

a. Pray specifically for the welfare of those you envy. Ask God to continue to bless them and enrich them.

b. Ask God to reveal your true riches to you. Family, friends, love, and most important, Jesus Himself.

c. Tell those you envy that you *admire* them: "I appreciate the abilities God has given you and I want you to know I pray that God will use you for His glory."

d. Believe that God will bring His richest blessings your way as you continue to serve Him.

Poison 3—What's That Lurking in Your Pantry? FEAR!!!: The first time I stayed alone I was filled with fear, listening to the creaking furnace and the swaying branches outside my window. Totally exhausted I fell asleep about three o'clock, only to be awakened by an old screen door falling down. My body tensed as the adrenalin shot through me and my heart pounded like a jack-hammer. I began to sweat and my head felt light, but as hard as I tried, I couldn't move. I barely breathed as I awaited my fate. By six in the morning it was beginning to get light, and I relaxed when nothing happened. At seven I called my dad to come and get me so I wouldn't spend another night paralyzed with fear. Since my husband has traveled most of our married life, it was clear I couldn't keep calling my father. I had to learn, like many others, to deal with fear.

Actually, fear is a healthy emotion, and God placed the adrenal system in us to alert and prepare us for *flight* or *fight* in danger. It would be foolish to walk upon a poisonous snake and kick at it with your bare foot. You are prepared internally to run or kill the snake. It would have been justifiable fear if a murderer had crawled through my window. But one didn't, and I was filled with un-justifiable fear.

Justifiable fear, programmed into us for protection, is from the Creator, but unjustifiable fear is from the enemy (Satan). "For God had not given us the spirit of fear; but of power, and of love, and of a sound mind" (2 Tim. 1:7). What does that mean practically? For me it is being able to sleep without a gun in my hand. It means when I awake abruptly at a loud noise and the adrenaline is pumping, I have to make a decision. I can either build a case of horror on the noise I heard, or I can say: "Satan, God has not given me a spirit of fear, He has given me the *ability* to fear danger. God has given me power and love and a sound mind. I am going to use that mind to quote verses that will put me back to sleep." The decision is mine, either succumb to unjustifiable fear or claim the security of God's Word and His protection.

These are some of the common fears of women:

a. Fear for husband's safety and life
b. Fear for children's safety and future
c. Fear of one's own future
d. Fear of being alone
e. Fear of pain and illness
f. Fear of poverty
g. Fear of speaking in public
h. Fear of death
i. Fear of your own husband (the battered wife)
j. Fear of going out among people

Christians, in trusting obedience to God's Word, can overcome these fears by taking the following steps:

1. Acknowledging unjustifiable fear as sin and repenting of it. This does not mean feeling guilty about the fear, but rather means making a decision to no longer willfully surrender to fear's illegitimate bondage over us.

2. Search the Scriptures for key promisory verses which contain God's assurances of confidence and protection for His children in every situation.

3. Prayer (asking God to help you break the fear habit).

4. Separating the fear *experience* from the fear *object*. You may have some justifiable fears of dangerous objects or situations. But the fear of an old (or imagined) event is an unjustifiable fear

because God is a God Who wishes to "continually make all things new."

5. Facing your fears with love and trust. If your fear is of elevators, you can only win by trusting God, getting into an elevator, and pushing the button. That sounds simple but I am aware that it is not, for people who have this fear, and some in-depth counseling may be needed to help you face your fears. Don't be afraid to ask for help, because countless thousands are facing fears too. God gave you the ability to fear to protect you, not so you would be enslaved to the spirit of fear!

 Poison 4—Depression, Despair, and Other Ropes for Hanging:

While Dr. Byrd has already discussed the details of depression, let's look at the *feeling* of depression.

I know the feeling as well as I know the back of my hand. I wish I could erase it from my memory, but just when I think I have, I come face to face with it in another woman, and I feel it all over again, for her.

I am gripped with remembrance when I see the hands and head hanging down, eyes don't sparkle or twinkle, and the lips have forgotten how to smile. There is a sadness for no apparent reason, a constant weariness. There is that "no hope" sighing and resignation.

I remember too well the food that turned to cotton wads as I chewed and choked trying to swallow. I remember clothes bagging and cheeks sinking in, the sleepless nights and the tearstained days when I cried for the darkness to come and swallow me up, only to then beg for the light of day.

I would say, "Well, I'm just a melancholic and I have to live with it." *What a lie!* I learned that I didn't have to live that way. I found that depression had affected my body, soul, and spirit, but what caused the depression? Was it just sin or did I have deep emotional problems that needed rooting out? Before I could deal, however, with the soul and the spirit, I had a physical being that needed attention. Under the care of a fine, Christian physician I found out some things about depression. I found out that while I felt like I was going crazy or losing my mind, depression does not mean that. What causes depression? We used to always think that unusual depression was caused by some conflict or hidden unhappiness in a person's life. While that and/or long illness or a death or divorce can lead to stress that precipitates depression, it need not be the cause. In fact, otherwise healthy people who have no reason to be unhappy can become depressed, too. I began to understand what Dr. Byrd explained earlier that most depression is caused by a deficiency of one or two special chemicals that carry messages from one nerve ending to the next, across the space between them, like little messengers. After delivering the message to the next nerve, they jump back to the nerve they came from. When enough messengers are there doing the job, no trouble occurs. But when there is a shortage of these chemical messengers, whatever that nerve transmission is supposed to do, it doesn't happen.

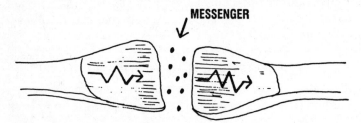

MESSENGER

When this deficiency occurred in my arm and leg as well as my eyes during a bout with multiple sclerosis, loss of motion or limitation of function took place.

When the deficiency of messengers occurs in the brain, the result is depression. While we don't always know why the special chemicals (messengers) that carry nerve impulses, become deficient, stress is often the culprit, as we saw earlier. There are now medicines available that correct the deficiency, either by preventing the chemical messengers from being further destroyed or by stopping their removal from the gap between nerves where they're supposed to do their jobs.

In other words, my doctor explained that the reason the medication he gave me was helping me recover from my depression was because I had been suffering a chemical imbalance in the brain, and antidepressant medication helped return brain chemistry to normal. I had been suffering clinical depression that wouldn't be corrected by counseling or prayer.

Slowly, very slowly I began to regain my ability to concentrate, make decisions, to study and get things done that looked too big before. The headache I had suffered with for years began subsiding. I began to feel less worthless, became enthusiastic again, and began to enjoy the simple things in life once more. I regained my appetite and the medication seemed to help my insomnia.

I am aware how new this is in certain Christian circles, and how some Christians would only attribute depression to sin. But as Dr. Byrd mentioned in chapter seven, sin is only one potential cause of depression. It's time we looked at the whole person. We must be aware that from time to time our emotions need medical help just as our physical bodies do.

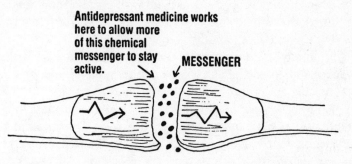

Antidepressant medicine works here to allow more of this chemical messenger to stay active.   MESSENGER

Depression and despair can weave a tight rope around your emotional neck, and will allow you to strangle yourself if not stopped. The book *Happiness Is a Choice* helped me to see that I had some choices to make. At any point in your "death row" experience you can give yourself a stay of execution. Because, you see, I *chose* a suicide attempt. It was wrong and sinful, but it was the natural conclusion to choosing depression as a way of life. We *do* have a choice. I wish I had listened to a family doctor who tried to treat me medically, but I thought antidepressants were sinful. I wish I had sought counseling before it went too far, but I didn't, and you know why? Pride! We should take pride in our work and our appearance; that kind of pride is healthy, but the ugly one that Satan hands us is not. Dr. Byrd has stated that 1) "false" guilt, 2) pride, and 3) lack of understanding are the three most common reasons that Christians neglect to get the medical treatment they need for a serious depression.

I didn't want any of the Christians I had taught or spoken to, to know I wasn't handling *my* life perfectly. I certainly didn't want unsaved people to think the God I had cheered and testified to wasn't able to meet *my* needs. I was more concerned about how I would look than finding a relief and being all God wanted me to be.

Why can't we see that being honest with each other about our hurts and failures might do more to speed on Christianity to those who need to hear than the false, "Being a Christian has solved all my problems" airs we put on. We find that when the jar cracks, something ugly may ooze out. If I said I've never had another blue day touched with the sadness of depression, I would be lying. I can say that I have chosen another way to deal with it.

My old way of dealing with it was to sit in my faded green rocker, wrapped in my faded green robe, read my ragged Bible, and beg God to take away the heaviness, the depression. For me God seemed to be saying, "Get up, get out." It often meant calling a friend, going to lunch or shopping, or maybe just riding in the mountains. While out in the fresh air taking the responsibility for my life, I had some of my most uplifting times of prayer and fellowship with the Lord. God met me as I left the seclusion of my room. If I were suffering clinical depression I would need medical help. But for minor depression, seeing the sun-kissed trees and people working in their yards or even the beautiful, new things in stores lets me know that in the world of situations, my problems are not earth-shattering. This too shall pass. When I return home (often with a bag or two), I have a proverbial "new lease" on life (and often an upcoming bill). Now, I'm aware that this solution is overly simplistic if you are involved with a divorce, a runaway child, severe pain, or chemotherapy. The point I want to make is that we *do* have choices about how we view, think about, work through, and react to our life problems. Whether we seek help from a minister, a counselor, or a doctor, it is imperative to seek help. We don't have to be depressed.

What about grief? Grief must not be confused with depression, although if indulged in too long, it can lead to depression. Grief is a real emotion, and if it is stifled the person may undergo severe emotional consequences later on. It can, for a time, be normal and healthy after a death, divorce, or other serious loss. But grief must be passed over and acceptance must occur. More and more people who have experienced grief say the best thing a visitor can do or say is nothing. Don't try to fill the painfully empty spaces with words. A person who will sit and not demand to be heard is a welcome comforter. The old adage, "Time heals," is usually true about grief, but not about depression. There is a need to *do* something to deal with depression.

 Poison 5—Worry: When my mother is worried about something, she says she can't think of anything else. She says it is like having a needle stuck on a record; she hears the same thing over and over. It may sound simple, but after years of worrying myself, my advice is to pick up the needle and move it. When we understand worry and the thought process, that is exactly the kind of control we have over it. People tell me they have hundreds of thoughts crowding into their minds and they can't seem to help worrying. We may have many thoughts crowding in but we are the ones who have to choose which thoughts to give consideration to. It is impossible to actually think of more than one thing at a time.

In the Bible the word *worry* is usually translated "anxiety" or "care." *Worry*, according to Webster, is: "A troubled state of mind, anxiety, distress; care; uneasiness. Something that causes anxiety or mental distress." Worry is actually concern over the future, maybe tomorrow, the next year, or even the next hour. Jesus knew some of the things we would worry over—food, clothing, and other daily needs and He said:

Therefore I tell you, stop being perpetually uneasy (anxious and worried) about your life, what you shall eat or what you shall drink, and about your body, what you shall put on. Is not life greater [in quality] than food, and the body [far above and more excellent] than clothing? (Matt. 6:25, AMPLIFIED.)

The Greek word in the New Testament for worry means "to divide, part, rip, or tear apart." It's like trying to describe the wind. You never actually see the wind, only the *results* of swaying branches. While you can't see the harmful emotion of worry, unless it is a wrinkled brow, you can certainly feel the effects.

There seems to be a very good explanation why we shouldn't spend our energies "being pulled apart" by worries of tomorrow.

1. There is nothing we can do about tomorrow since it hasn't been given to us yet. It still belongs to Christ.
2. We will need all our energies working out the troubles or problems Christ says we have today. And we do have them.

It would be foolish for me as a mother to see my crying, hungry child and pass by my refrigerator that holds today's supply of food and go out to buy food for tomorrow. It is the same principle. God has given us the grace to deal with one day at a time, and we must not waste that grace worrying about tomorrow.

That is not to say that we shouldn't plan for the future in a responsible manner; we should. But we are to focus our energies primarily on serving the Lord with confidence today.

We have a clear choice of whether to worry or not. Philippians 4:4–7 gives us four rules that, if followed, will cause us to trade worries in for the corresponding fruit of the Spirit, peace:

a. Rejoice in the Lord. Praise Him. (Say thank You.)
b. Let your moderation be known. (Learn self-control.)
c. Be careful for nothing. (Yield your anxiety and worry to God.)
d. By prayer, with thanksgiving, let your request be made

known unto God. (Simply talk to the Lord about what you want Him to do.)

The payoff is peace, the peace of God which passeth all understanding.

We have touched on some of the poisons in our emotional pantry. Summarized in the chart below is an expanded list of these "poisons" and the choices we can make to overcome them by practicing the fruit of the Spirit.

Emotional Poisons and Corresponding Fruit of the Spirit
(from Galatians 5:22–23)

1. Fear	1. *Love* (trust grounded in faith)
2. Depression, despair	2. *Joy* (His promises becoming our hope)
3. Worry, anxiety	3. *Peace* (His presence becoming our shield)
4. A complaining, "pushy" attitude	4. *Patience* (an even-temper under fire)
5. Anger, hostility	5. *Kindness* (returning good for evil)
6. Impurity	6. *Goodness* (seeking to be holy, for He is holy)
7. Dishonesty, unreliability	7. *Faithfulness* (dependability at all cost)
8. Bitterness, resentment	8. *Gentleness* (forgiveness and compassion)
9. Impulsiveness, self-gratification	9. *Self-control* (setting aside the desires of the flesh for the goals of the Spirit)

Study Questions

1. Discuss the three ways we generally handle anger.
2. Name three types of anger and discuss with the group which is more troublesome to you and what the biblical response is.

3. What sequence does Christ give us in Matthew 18:15–17 for resolving our differences with an offended brother or sister?
4. Do you agree that greed and jealousy stem from a lack of contentment? Discuss.
5. Discuss the difference between healthy, justifiable fear and unhealthy, unjustifiable fear.
6. Name five steps for overcoming fear.
7. Has the discussion of neurotransmitters or chemical messengers helped you understand depression better?
8. What four rules will cause us to trade worries for peace of mind? (Phil. 4:4–7)

Chapter 10
Exercising the Soul

"Soul Sweat"

The soul requires exercise just as the body does. Unlike the body, which is exercised by the laws of physical exertion, the soul is exercised through certain laws governing our involvement in the lives of others. These laws of involvement necessarily take the form of practical actions and relationships. Four of the most vital of these laws of involvement required to properly exercise the soul are:

Law I.   Giving and serving—God's law of return on our investments.
Law II. Developing activities which renew one's zest and motivation for daily living.
Law III. Cultivating friendships which "pay off" in interpersonal genuineness.
Law IV. Building better marriages.

Law I: *Giving and serving—God's law of return on our investments.* Christ stated in Mark 10:45, "For even the Son of Man did not come to be served, but to serve, and to give His life a ransom for many" (NASB). Indeed, God does promise both temporal and eternal returns on the monies which we invest for the propagation of the gospel. Luke 6:38 says, " 'Give, and it will be given to you; good measure, pressed down, shaken together, running over, they will pour into your lap. For whatever measure you deal out to others, it will be dealt to you in return' " (NASB). Any successful businessman will tell you that God has honored that principle time and time again in His financial dealings with others. It is a well-known and true statement that "he is no fool who gives what he cannot keep to gain that which he cannot lose." Although the concept of giving is certainly dealt with extensively in the New Testament, the concept of serving is even more extensively covered.

Serving is the unconditional meeting of another person's needs without expectation of personal return. The Christian concept of serving is in many ways an antithesis of the world's motto of "get all you can, and get ahead." In the world's system, the task of serving is often relegated to the youngest members of organization. But in Christianity, the Scriptures tell us that serving is a task which marks maturity. " 'But not so with you, but let him who is the greatest among you become as the youngest and the leader as the servant' " (Luke 22:26, NASB). Many individuals will attest that they are quite willing to serve others when the opportunity presents itself, whereas, as Christians we are told to be out among the people of the world looking for occasions to serve. Christ described Himself as One Who was among the masses with the intention of serving (Luke 22:27).

The true servant of God, functioning effectively within the body of Christ, will have certain characteristics indicative of his lifestyle. There are at least seven characteristics of the Christian servant.

Characteristic 1: The servant prizes the interests of others *above his own* and by doing so obeys the command of Scripture in Philippians 2:3–4 (NASB),

> Do nothing from selfishness or empty conceit, but with humility of mind let each of you regard one another as more important than himself; do not merely look out for your own personal interest, but also for the interest of others.

Characteristic 2: Servants go where the needs are and do not necessarily serve simply where it is convenient or comfortable. Christ was very explicit in His words to His disciples when it came to explaining the fact that the servant must be wherever the master sends him. John 12:26 (NASB) says, "'If anyone serves Me, let him follow Me; and where I am, there shall My servant also be.'"

Characteristic 3: The servant understands the "billboard principle." We are told to be a living display to the glory of God. Isaiah 49:3 (NASB) says, "You are My servant, Israel, in Whom I will show My glory." For most people, the only gospel they will ever see is the picture of Christ they see being lived in the lives of Christians. "Whether, then, you eat or drink or whatever you do, do all to the glory of God," (1 Cor. 10:31, NASB).

Characteristic 4: The servant understands that the yielding of personal rights and privileges is foundational to the attitude of the true servant. In describing Christ, Paul says that although He was the Son of God Himself, He did not consider equality with God as something to be grasped (or taken advantage of), but instead made Himself humble to the point of serving others. We must be as willing to forgo our own special interests in meeting the needs of others.

Characteristic 5: The servant is willing to forfeit his personal liberty in order to have access to serving others. The Apostle Paul tells us not to use our freedom as sons and daughters of Jesus Christ to merely indulge our own interests in this life, but rather to use this freedom as an opportunity to seek out and meet the needs of others. "Do not turn your freedom into an opportunity for the flesh, but through love serve one another" (Gal. 5:13, NASB).

Sometimes serving others in love requires a tremendous sacrifice in personal liberty. There is a story told of a group of missionaries in the 1800s seeking to minister to the slaves on an island off the coast of South America. Because of the large number of slaves on the island and the harshness of the living conditions, the plantation owners feared the gospel message and its possible results. Thus, they would not allow the missionaries to even talk with the slaves. They would only allow other slaves to talk with their slaves. In an act of supreme unselfishness, the missionaries decided to sell themselves into slavery on the island in order to be able to take gospel to the native slaves there. What an incredible cost they paid for the privilege of serving those people, and yet, many converts were won as a result of the testimony of these courageous Christian servants.

Characteristic 6: The servant will serve his enemies at a time when others would only be willing to serve friends. Christ describes the difficulty which will be involved in serving an enemy at an inopportune time. He makes the point that even the lost people of this world understand returning kindness for kindness; and yet it is only the Christian who can consistently and sincerely return good for evil. "If you lend to those from whom you expect to receive, what credit is that to you? Even sinners lend to sinners, in order to receive back the same amount. But love your enemies, and do good, and lend, expecting nothing in return; and your reward will be great, and you will be sons of the Most High; for He Himself is kind to ungrateful and evil men" (Luke 6:34–35, NASB).

Characteristic 7: The servant sees the big picture. She understands that the overall objective of the Christian is to glorify God and thereby attain the final victory where Christ will say, "Well done, good and faithful servant." The servant understands that her responsibility and privilege is to have the aroma of a personal knowledge of Jesus Christ emanating from her at all times (2 Corinthians 2:14).

Law II: *Developing activities which renew one's zest and motivation for daily living.* Certainly the drudgery of carrying out the day-to-day responsibilities of life can at times become almost overpowering to even the most committed Christian. How can a Christian remain personally enthusiastic and sharp in a world filled with endless requirements and obligations? The only way is to develop a series of well-ordered priorities involving the distribution of *time, money,* and *strength.* The order of priorities which we feel to be scripturally most sound is as follows:

First: Daily personal relationship with Jesus Christ including reasonable physical care for the health, exercise, and fitness of the body as the temple of the Holy Spirit.

Second: Relationship with spouse.

Third: Relationship with children.

Fourth: Relationship with close family members outside the immediate family.

Fifth: Relationship to ministry, that is, those individuals whom God has given us the privilege of discipling. These may be other couples or individual Christians we are seeking to equip in both skills and character qualities. This involves imparting our life to such individuals, and ideally this occurs within the context of our involvement in a local church.

Sixth: Vocation (work, career, schooling).

Seventh: Other activities, including church-related activities, and leisure time pursuits.

One of the things which we often encourage Christians to do on a weekly basis is to set aside some "buzz" time for activities which they simply find fulfilling as a source of enjoyment. Although such activities may not contribute directly to the higher priorities just mentioned above, they do serve as an overall source of rejuvenation and encouragement. The following is a list of 131 different activities which are potentially available as so-called "buzz" time pursuits. We would encourage you to look over this list and see if there's some activity you could do during the week which would prove enjoyable and be an encouragement to you. You'll find your spouse and family members are usually more than willing to assist you in setting aside some personal time to involve yourself in one or more of these activities. Oftentimes, others realize better than we do just how much more we have to give out when we have taken time to replenish our own reserves.

Check the ones which you might find potentially find interesting and enjoyable.

__ Cooking/ Baking	__ Working on cars	__ Bowling
__ Cake decorating	__ Model building	__ Softball
__ Collecting (coins, stamps)	__ Aquariums	__ Basketball
__ Macramé	__ Batik/Tie-dyeing	__ Football
__ Pottery/ Ceramics	__ Silkscreening	__ Soccer
__ Drawing/ Sketching	__ Printing	__ Shuffleboard
__ Photography	__ Copper enameling	__ Watching sports
__ Sewing	__ String art	__ Rugby
__ Leather work	__ Church clubs	__ Tennis
__ Home decorating	__ Garden clubs	__ Golf
__ Flower arranging	__ Jaycees	__ Judo/Karate
__ Metal work	__ Folk dance	__ Racquetball
__ Woodworking	__ Ballet	__ Snorkeling/ Scuba diving
__ Decoupage	__ Films	__ Auto racing
__ Stained glass	__ Stage shows	__ Flying
__ Mosaic tile work	__ Opera	__ Hunting
	__ Play reading	__ Hang gliding
	__ Community theatre	__ Parachuting
	__ Charades	__ Roller-skating
	__ Swimming	__ Billiards
		__ Chess
		__ Checkers

__ Candlemaking
__ Jewelry making
__ Sculpturing
__ Film making
__ Restoring antiques
__ Knitting/ Crocheting
__ Needlework
__ Ping-pong
__ Hiking
__ Backpacking
__ Camping
__ Picnics
__ Bird watching
__ Horseback riding
__ Bicycling
__ Motorcycling
__ Sightseeing
__ Caving (spelunking)
__ Outdoor cooking
__ Canoeing
__ Orienteering
__ Mountain climbing
__ Trailer camping
__ Social clubs
__ Singing
__ Attending parties/ Fellowships
__ Attending lectures

__ Jogging/ Running
__ Badminton
__ Volleyball
__ Sailing
__ Water skiing
__ Snow skiing
__ Fishing
__ Archery
__ "Bull sessions"/Discussion groups
__ Visiting friends, relatives
__ Belonging to a political group
__ Attending crafts fairs
__ Gardening
__ House plants
__ Keeping pets
__ Combing beach for objects
__ Nature walks
__ Rock collecting
__ Dart throwing
__ Wild flower, plant identification
__ Piano
__ Singing groups
__ Guitar
__ Listening to music

__ Board games (Life, Monopoly)
__ Card games
__ Video games/ Pinball
__ Lawn games (Croquet, Horseshoes)
__ Playing any instrument
__ Watching TV
__ Sunbathing
__ Sleeping
__ Reading
__ Crossword puzzles
__ Volunteer work
__ Traveling
__ Listening to radio
__ Aerobic dancing
__ Going shopping
__ Kite flying
__ Talking on telephone
__ Creative writing
__ Writing poetry
__ Writing letters
__ Relaxation training

Law III: *Cultivating friendships which "pay off" in interpersonal genuineness.* It has been said that friendships are easy to start and yet tough to maintain. I believe this is a very true statement. We all have had the experience of beginning a friendship with the very best of intentions and under the best of circumstances, only to have that friendship erode over time. The primary cause of erosion in friendships and the resulting interpersonal pain is the difficulty which friends often have in resolving conflicts. By its very nature, friendship involves the coming together in mutual positive regard of two different and distinct individuals. Each person has her own values, opinions, wants, wishes, fears, and attitudes. In the text that follows we will look at how to handle situations when friends disagree.

1. *Do not get into the habit of judging others.*

Engaging in such judging either puts the Christian in danger of becoming *critical* (feeling that another person is worse than you), or of becoming *contemptuous* (feeling that you are better than another person). Either of these two postures is unacceptable to the Lord and poisonous to a friendship. In Matthew 7:3–6, Christ says we are to spend the majority of our energy examining our own lives before we comment on someone else's.

2. *Make every effort to keep unity within the body of Christ.*

In Ephesians 4:1–3, Paul stresses the responsibility which we all have as Christians to live in harmony with our brothers and sisters. He states that such unity and harmony is one of the hallmarks of being a Christian. Resolving a contention with a fellow Christian is not an option, it is a command from the Lord if we are to maintain a close and worthy walk with Him.

3. *Don't miss the point.*

The purpose of friendships, the purpose of the fellowship of the church, and the purpose of being placed in one body is to bring glory to the head of that body, Jesus Christ. The privilege of being bound together with other saved saints is a benefit which the Lord wants us to enjoy, and it is a responsibility which He expects us to properly carry out. As Christians we do not have the option of being angry or bitter over a period of time toward another Christian. Sure, the sting of a personal offense at the hands of another Christian cannot be ignored, and in fact, it may leave some emotional "soreness" until a reconciliation can occur. But to allow a matter of disagreement or inner hurt to continually "sting" our personality with prolonged bitterness is to invite the chronic spiritual blood poisoning of alienation from God and reproach from our fellow Christians.

Law IV: *Build better marriages:* Many books have been written on the subject of Christian marriage, and rightfully so. Possibly no other institution on earth has more to do with the eventual stability and health of the church than Christian homes and marriages. In the text below we will look at one means of improving general communication and understanding within marriage.

Any successful businessman knows that in order to make wise decisions for the future, he must take an inventory of that business on a regular basis. Likewise, a wise marriage partner will want to take a regular inventory of the status of his or her marriage. Below is an inventory which we recommend couples to complete monthly. It's called the "State of the Union" Inventory, and it provides for the gathering of some useful information by each marriage partner.

"State of the Union" Inventory

1. Look at these two lists, then rate each item as to how significant it is in causing disunity in your marriage.

F = Frequently causes conflict
O = Occasionally causes conflict
R = Rarely (or never) causes conflict

Situations	Qualities
__ Unfulfilled needs/ disappointments	__ Unwillingness to communicate

__ Fatigue
__ Work pressures
__ Financial difficulties or
   disagreements
__ Health problems
__ Busy schedule
__ Family background or
   upbringing
__ Relatives or neighbors
__ Lack of spiritual growth
   or differences of opinion
   on religious matters
__ Difficulties or disagree-
   ments concerning the
   children

__ _____

__ Critical or sarcastic
   comments
__ Jumping to conclusions
__ Being inflexible
   (or stubborn)
__ Being impulsive
__ Nagging
__ Being insensitive
__ Laziness
__ Annoying personal
   habits
__ Rude or tactless
   behavior

__ _____

2. Three things that please me which my mate does:
   1.
   2.
   3.
3. Three strengths that I admire in my mate:
   1.
   2.
   3.
4. Three things which I know please him/her:
   1.
   2.
   3.
5. One aspect of my behavior I would like to change:

6. Three things I would like my spouse to do more often:
   1.
   2.
   3.
7. One thing he/she does that irritates me:

8. Note: How and when can I best communicate this?
   a. How?
   b. When?
9. How would I like him/her to request changes in my behavior?

Unfortunately, there is a negative side to the marriage relationship; that is, there are stages of deterioration which can occur when the level of communication and intimacy erodes. Each stage is more serious than the one preceding it. No stage is hopeless, but quality marital counseling from a trained pastor or Christian counselor is often required to rebuild a seriously struggling marriage. If you identify your marriage as being in one of these stages, then make it your urgent priority to find a way back to quality communication and intimacy.

Stage One—The Disillusionment Stage

The disillusionment stage marks the end of the fantasies which each partner may have had about the other prior to marriage. This stage may begin after a year or two of marriage, and instead of becoming discouraged, it is important for each spouse to realize that God has carefully matched them as a couple so that one's "blind" spots are another's "sensitive" spots. The weaknesses of one's spouse are inevitably the other's strengths. The couple must realize that it is *commitment* and not *compatibility* which is the first foundation stone of the marriage. When there is a deep level of commitment to the marriage by each spouse, then the couple can truly begin the process of understanding and utilizing their points of personality difference to become more flexible and well-rounded. If God hadn't mixed many of us so-called "opposites" in marriage, He would have missed one of His most fruitful opportunities to force us out of our old, stale personality patterns and into fresh, new ones. God likes to use the stress of the marriage relationship to stretch and develop us as we journey along our pilgrimage to spiritual maturity.

Stage Two—The Erosion Stage

The erosion stage is when the simple irritations of the disillusionment stage begin to take the form of direct attack on the character and personality of one's mate. It is in this stage that the husband and wife begin to lose real confidence in one another.

Stage Three—The Isolation Stage

The highly charged emotions and sometimes angry fighting of the erosion stage now give way to a form of icy silence. Feelings seem to die and are replaced by apathy. It has been said that the opposite of love is not hate, but indifference; and indeed the isolation stage is marked by progressive emotional detachment. The words "I love you" have all but ceased to be a part of the couple's conversation.

Stage Four—The "I Don't Care Anymore" Stage

In this stage the anger, hurt, humiliation, and frustration of the earlier stages have given way to a sense of hopeless apathy. Interest in the marriage as a fulfilling relationship has essentially vanished on the part of both spouses, and neither one can see a reasonable way for the marriage to survive. In this period, each spouse repeatedly weighs the cost of dissolving the marriage against the emotional cost of trying to piece it back together. The couple may feel like strangers living in the same home, and making even the simplest of decisions together is a strain, causing friction.

Stage Five—The Separation Stage

When a couple moves out from living together, it is one of the most intensely stressful events of a lifetime. Rapid mood swings from silliness (a false sense of euphoria) to absolute despondency often follow within the course of a few weeks. Feelings of embarrassment, guilt, revenge, jealousy, and insecurity flow like an avalanche over each of them. There are many questions and fears about just what configuration life will take on from this point forward.

Stage Six—The Grief or Mourning Stage

In this stage, the couple has truly given up hope that the marriage can be salvaged. Symbolic behaviors such as no longer wearing the wedding band or separating socially from old married friends are indicative of this stage. In this stage a person will often either appear stunned (largely immobilized and seemingly unable to make decisions) or on the other hand, they will attempt to give the appearance of security by rushing about in a flurry of action and socially gregarious activities. All of this comes about as an attempt to forestall a sense of loneliness and personal failure.

Stage Seven—The "Second Childhood" Stage

Once a divorce is imminent, and the two marriage partners are living separately, one or both may return to many behaviors reminiscent of adolescence. Impulsive decisions, extravagant spending, alcohol and drug abuse, sexual promiscuity, and a general carelessness about life may begin to appear in this stage. Such behavior is the person's final defense against the hopeless discouragement of having been involved in the disintegration of a marriage. Even at this late stage, two willing parties can still accomplish a reconciliation and a rebirth of a good marriage.

Stage Eight—Divorce

Even though a divorce may have occurred, it is still God's wish to see a couple reconcile and reconstitute their marriage. If this is utterly impossible, then the process of working through the trauma of the postdivorce period must go forward. As great a tragedy as divorce is, it is the responsibility of the church to uphold, encourage, and equip such individuals through forgiveness and instruction as they seek to serve the Lord once again.

Study Questions

1. Discuss some of the seven characteristics of a Christian servant.
2. How do you feel about the list of priorities under Law II?
3. How many "buzz" time activities (things you do for yourself) could you check?
4. Discuss the three steps to follow when friends disagree.
5. Did you do the "State of the Union" Inventory? How did you feel about it?
6. At which of the eight stages of deterioration can a marriage be saved? How?

Chapter 11
Clothing the Soul

Dressed for Battle

The Christian life can be described in many ways but certainly one of the most accurate descriptions is that it is a battle. In his letter to the Ephesian church, Paul describes the life of the Christian as a battle against the might of Satan. Interestingly, he spends a large portion of the sixth chapter of Ephesians, not describing the manner of warfare, but rather describing the proper armor in which the Christian must dress himself daily in order to be capable of fighting effectively (Eph. 6:10–17, NASB). In beginning his discussion of the soul's armor, Paul gives us the two objectives of the spiritual struggle. *Objective #1:* To stand firm, resisting Satan "in the evil day." This objective of standing firm or remaining faithful in the midst of struggle requires an attitude of faithfulness, an attitude of motivation toward becoming all that we can in Christ Jesus. *Objective #2:* To see clearly the "schemes of the devil." Our concepts regarding the devil and his intentions must be accurate so that we may properly equip ourselves. Interestingly,

Paul's description of the six articles of the soul's armor divide evenly into two categories: (1) three articles are *beliefs*, and (2) three articles are *attitudes*; we must have these beliefs and attitudes in order to be well-equipped Christians. First, we will look at the three articles of the soul's armor that deal with our beliefs.

Article 1 "Stand firm therefore, having girded your loins of truth." The first component of the soul's armor is the "girdle of truth." The first century Roman soldier protected his loins or lower abdomen with a large belt which was cinched tightly and upon which the rest of the armor depended for several reasons. There were at least three important functions which the large belt or girdle served in the battle dress of the soldier.

The first function of the belt was to secure the rest of the armor in place. All of the major components of the armor were either attached to or designed to rest firmly against the belt. The breast plate, the sword, and even the shield depended upon the belt for attachment or reinforcement. In the same way, the truth girds or strengthens the mind of the Christian for action. Without the underlying security of knowing the truth about Jesus Christ, the rest of the armor has no firm foundation upon which to rest. 1 Peter 1:13 commands us to "gird up the loins of your mind" for action.

A second function of the belt in the soldier's armor was to make available the rest of the armor for proper use. It was the breast plate's attachment to the belt which kept it in place to be available for protection of the chest in all positions, and it was to the stable belt that the sword was attached for support and availability in all situations. Likewise, it is the truth about the doctrines in the Christian faith which maintains our readiness or availability as Christians to deal with the many situations which we face. Luke 12:35 says literally "let your loins be girded about" with readiness.

The third function of the belt in the soldier's armor was to allow him freedom of movement. The belt served its functions well, but did not impair the flexibility of the soldier in adopting many different positions to meet varying circumstances. So, too, it is the great truths of the Christian faith which free the Christian from the bondage of legalism and allow him to serve the Lord openly and with the freedom to follow his own conscience under the guidelines of the Holy Spirit and the Word of God. In describing the liberty which the Christian has who truly knows the truth of Jesus Christ, the Lord says in John 8:32: "And ye shall know the truth, and the truth shall make you free."

Article 2 "And having shod your feet with the preparation of the gospel of peace." The next article which the Christian must have in his armor in order to be prepared for the day's battle is the preparation of the gospel. This preparation of the gospel is compared to the footwear of the Roman soldier because the sandals which he wore were bound by thongs over the instep and around the ankle. The soles were thickly studded with nails. This gave the Roman soldier firm footing in virtually every situation and enabled him to be perpetually prepared for an attack. For the Christian, it is our preparation of the gospel which allows us to be ready to deal with the many situations which we face. This preparation is not the study of the Word of God, for that is involved in the girding of ourselves with the truth as mentioned above. Rather, it is our preparing the hearts of the nonChristians to receive the message of Jesus Christ. The gospel is prepared for reception in the hearts of the nonbelievers by the lifestyles of those who claim to be Christians. It has been said that a nonChristian must first see Christianity *in* you before he will accept it *from* you. See 2 Corinthians 3: 2–3.

Article 3 "And take the helmet of salvation." The third component of the soul's armor dealing with the beliefs of the Christian has to do with the matter of salvation. In the soldier's armor, it is the helmet which protects the head or the brain. The brain is the relay center through which all information must pass, and also it is the brain which sends commands for action to every limb. An injury to the head can completely immobilize the body, and accordingly, an injury to the believer's confidence in his salvation can absolutely immobilize him for effective service to the Lord. John 10:27–29 says that nothing can dislodge the Christian from God's protective hand.

Now, let's look at the three components of the soul's armor that deal with attitudes which the Christian soldier must possess.

Article 4 "Having put on the breastplate of righteousness." The purpose of the breastplate in the soldier's armor was to protect his chest, and specifically his heart. An injury directly to the heart was thought to be the quickest way to die in battle. And indeed, an injury to the righteousness of our lives is the quickest way to kill the quality of our relationship with the Lord. Hebrews 10:22 says that we are to draw near to the Lord with a sincere heart full of assurance, having cleansed ourselves with our hearts from an evil conscience, and in James 4:8, the Christian is told to draw near to the Lord, cleansing our hands and purifying our hearts in order that we may be able to truly understand the privilege of personally knowing God. We must, as Christians, determine that we are going to daily seek to bring our lives into closer and closer conformity with the life of Jesus Christ. The benefits of such a decision and a lifestyle committed to holiness are many, but in the context of spiritual warfare, the primary benefit is the attitude of courage and confidence which comes from right living. Proverbs 28:1 (NASB) says that "the wicked flee when no one is pursuing, but the righteous are bold as a lion." The attribute (or attitude) of courage is absolutely essential for the proper waging of Christian warfare, and it is dependent for its existence upon a heart committed to righteous living.

Article 5 "In addition to all, taking up the shield of faith with which you will be able to extinguish the flaming missiles of the evil one." In the armor of the first century soldier, it was his shield which stood between him and the spears and flaming arrows of the enemy. In like fashion, an attitude of faith (the confident belief in the willingness and the ability of God to act on behalf of His children) enables the Christian to withstand the onslaughts of evil. In the day-to-day battle of living the Christian life, it is fear which opposes an attitude of faith. Abraham, a true man of faith, was given some words by the Lord which influenced the rest of his life. "Do not fear, Abram, I am a shield to you; your reward shall be very great" (Genesis 15:1, NASB).

Article 6 "And the sword of the Spirit, which is the word of God." The sword was the offensive weapon which the soldier had at his disposal in battle. Hebrews 4:12 also identifies that magnificent "sword of the spirit" as the Word of God. The sword of the spirit (or the Word of God) has many uses in the hands of a mature Christian; however, its most vital role may well be to prepare the attitude of the Christian for each day's spiritual battle. As we look closely at the text in Ephesians 6:17, we see that it is the sword of the Spirit, the Word of God, which must be utilized daily in the following three ways:

1. *Memorize* what it says (Psalm 119:11).
2. *Meditate* on how it fits in my innermost personality (Joshua 1:8).
3. *Mobilize* and do what the Word of God says (James 1:22).

To be the fully equipped soldier that God would have us to be, we must see to it that our souls are fully "dressed for battle" each day. The temptation to get discouraged and let the distractions of hectic modern living overcome us are great, but the rewards of being properly equipped to "win" the day's battle for the Lord are much greater!

Study Questions

1. Do you agree with the authors that the Christian life is a battle? How so in your life?
2. What are the two objectives of the spiritual struggle?
3. What three articles of the soul's armor deal with our beliefs? Discuss.
4. Are non-believers attracted by your lifestyle to Jesus Christ?
5. Which three components of the soul's armor deal with our attitudes?
6. According to Article 4, what is the quickest way to kill the quality of our relationship with the Lord?
7. Name three ways the Word of God must be utilized daily.

Keeping Out the Riff-Raff

What about the harmful critters of the soul? Where do they gather? Can we be free of them?

I want you to think of the mind as a gym where harmful critters assemble. You must know that it is there, in the mind, where you must work out to restore a healthy, happy thought life. The verse "As a man thinketh in his heart so is he" is the key to control.

It will take work to restore your thought life and emotional sweat to fight ugly bulges of wrong thinking, but the results are worth it.

Sweets were the stronghold that kept fat on my waist, but finding the stronghold emotionally was more difficult. A prominent preacher once described the process as follows:

A stronghold starts with a thought;
A thought becomes an idea;
An idea becomes an attitude;
Attitude becomes an action;
Action, if repeated, becomes a habit, and
Habit becomes a STRONGHOLD.

My own stronghold began with negative thoughts about the goodness of God as it related to my poor health.

Imagine with me that we are looking inside our heads at our gym and we see a balance beam, treadmill, weights, and other devices for getting us into shape. As owner of the gym, we may refuse admittance to any client (thought) we wish. We know it would be better business if we kept out the riff-raff of fear, anger, jealousy, worry, and depression. To do this most effectively, we must run the door ourselves.

When the client (thought) "Self-pity" knocked at my door and said, "You poor dear, God has been awfully hard on you," I should have put my foot to his backside. When I didn't, the thought became *idea*. When I didn't boot him out, his friend Anger knocked and said, "You have worked so hard for God and look what you get in return, sickness and pain." Once they were in the gym with me we took turns on the balance beam until the muscles of the *attitude* were strong; then they turned into depression and despair. Day after day, moment by moment, I observed these clients flex their muscles and walk the treadmill going nowhere except the "Despair Depot." I got into the habit of thinking that suicide was the only answer, and that led to the suicide *action*. Months of suicide thinking produced a *habit*. Even after the attempt, when I looked into the gym it seemed empty except for the *stronghold* of suicide thinking.

I remember telling the doctors that I didn't know why I was depressed. When I decided that I really wanted to be restored, I had some decisions to make. I had to march into my gym and take control again by:

1. Acknowledging the spiritual warfare. I couldn't regain control without a battle because the enemy was camped there (not demon possession, but oppression).

2. Identifying the stronghold. It took some time, as I shared in another chapter, before I discovered the wrong reaction to anger as the stronghold.

3. Identifying the source of the stronghold. The source was Satan, and yet the stronghold itself was made up of emotions, ideas, and attitudes which I had erroneously accepted as being true

about myself. These very emotions, ideas, and attitudes were the psychological (mental) "flab" which had joined together in my mind to become a stronghold of negativism and doubt. Satan was using my own emotions and self-concepts as a stronghold against me.

4. Deciding on a psychological "fitness" program. As I assessed the gym and the emotions and ideas working out there, I realized I must do what I did physically. I had to set a goal towards restoration and find a program to achieve it. I knew that my program would need to start as soon as possible in order to begin dissolving these inner mental strongholds. My goal was a healthy mind that could receive healthy emotional stimuli and reject the harmful. I wanted to be rid of excess baggage. My individual achievement program was set up as follows.

How to Win at Mental Gymnastics

To understand that our life's battles are won or lost in our minds, look at these verses:

> Unto the pure all things are pure: but unto them that are defiled and unbelieving is nothing pure; but even their mind and conscience is defiled (Titus 1:15).

> The thoughts of the wicked are an abomination to the Lord; but the words of the pure are pleasant words (Prov. 15:26).

> Because the carnal mind is enmity against God: for it is not subject to the law of God, neither indeed can be (Rom. 8:7).

A noble and Christlike character is not a thing of chance or favor, but the result of continued, consistent exercise in right thinking. In the gym of the mind, the muscles that are built can create a shapely character or a distorted one. That character can be gowned in peace and joy or bound by ropes of fear and misery. The choice is ours. Whom do we let in the gym, and what kind of program has been planned? We are masters over our own minds. But as we enter the gym to clean it, negative thoughts will continue jumping on the balance beam to exercise. The battle begins, but while we are masters, we must not fight the enemy in the flesh. Look at the exercise plan:

> For the weapons of our warfare are not carnal, but mighty through God to the pulling down of strong holds; casting down imaginations, and every high thing that exalteth itself against the knowledge of God, and bringing into captivity every thought to the obedience of Christ; and having a readiness to revenge all disobedience, when your obedience is fulfilled (2 Cor. 10:4–6).

Armed with spiritual weapons such as the sword of the Spirit and God's Word, try to visualize yourself *pulling down* the *stronghold* thought from the balance beam and replacing it with a godly thought. The next move is to *cast down imaginations* and the conceited things that exalt themselves against the truth of God's written Word to you. In your knowledge of God, you know He says, "I love you." But Satan says, "God can't love you; look what He did to you." Which of these two thoughts will you allow to exercise in your gym?

Imaginations may be the strongest enemy we have. See Genesis 6:5; Proverbs 6:16, 18; Ezekiel 8:12; and Romans 1:21.

Our Maker understood what the mind could do for either good or evil. Our mind is a gift given in love, and we must assume responsibility. One mind expands with beauty and art. Another, thinking the chambers of his imagery to be dark, fantasizes and gives in to lustful, covetous thinking, and rapists, thieves, and murderers are born. In order to have the freedom of the one mind to make a symphony, we must take the chance on the freedom of the other. Which will it be for you?

How many times have we given in to despair when a teenager is twenty minutes late getting home? We feel grief and cry hot tears of sadness when all of a sudden he drives up the driveway, unharmed. Imagination!

As we imagine ourselves thin and becoming lovelier by the

minute, we also have the power in that dark mystery-land to imagine our female competitor losing her teeth and going bald! We may snicker at such harmless exercises; but are they indeed harmless?

Once I understood the stronghold principle while I was recuperating after the suicide attempt, I realized suicidal thinking was a habit. I was trying to understand how to use the Word of God as a weapon one day, when before I knew it, up on the balance beam was this thought, "You better kill yourself, you will never make it, you big failure!"

I was reading the Bible at the time, John 10, enjoying the new knowledge for me about the ministry of the Good Shepherd, when the thought exalted itself against the knowledge of God. I was discouraged that I wasn't seeming to gain much ground. I wanted to be free, but how? Tears formed a pool on the open page of my Bible and I reached for a tissue to wipe up the little pool when my eyes fell on John 10:10 and the Lord seemed to urge me, saying, "This is your weapon, use it."

> The thief cometh not, but for to steal, and to kill, and to destroy; I am come that they might have life, and that they might have it more abundantly.

In an instant, restoration of my mind began when I said, "Satan, these thoughts are not God's nor mine, they are yours and I refuse them. Jesus said He came to give life more abundantly and I want to live." That verse dealt Satan a painful blow and he has never brought that thought back to my gym to exercise. He tries by other means to gain admittance, and I must ever be alert to his tactics.

Why didn't God just chase him away for me when I prayed? It was a long time before I understood that. God is teaching me to be an overcomer! "Be not overcome with evil, but overcome evil with good" (Rom. 12:21). "For whatsoever is born of God overcometh the world: and this is the victory that overcometh the world, even our faith" (1 John 5:4). "Resist the devil, and he will flee from you" (James 4:7).

Emotional Walking

While going to a gym or an exercise class is dramatic enough to show you mean business about firming up, walking is effective exercise. It is something you can do rain or shine. Emotionally speaking, it is the consistent, steady walking with God that gets little attention, but helps more than we ever know. There were many things I didn't understand until I had walked with Him awhile. There are many more things I won't understand until I walk some more with Him. There are many things we have no right to say until we have walked with Him. On my physical walk every day, I see new handiworks that I hadn't noticed before—the scent of a magnolia or lilac bush that brushes my nostrils with sweetness. On my daily walk with Him I find stability and the sweetness of strength needed to be healthy emotionally.

If you just walked on Sunday, you would hardly notice the difference or even call it exercise. Spiritually and emotionally, the same is true. If you just walked in the Christian life on Sunday, you are in the Lord, but the strength, growth, and stability will be weak.

Yesterday I put on a warm down jacket for my walk in the snow-covered street. When I reached certain spots where the sun was shining, the snow was melting and I had to unbutton the jacket because it was warmer than I thought, especially after the increased circulation.

I was reminded of how the enemy of my soul warns me not to venture too far out in my spiritual walk for fear of the cold or the hardness. If I heed him not and walk on, I will surely see he has lied, and the walk is not nearly so painful once my emotional circulation is improved by the steady pumping of my heart.

Lynchburg is called the City of Seven Hills, but when I'm walking it seems like seventy times seven. In our spiritual walk we have hills to climb, and if we stand at the bottom thinking we can't make it, we sap our own strength. Christ is at the top, cheering us on, offering a hand when the climbing gets rough.

Recently on my walk a big black dog began growling and barking as I got close to his house. My heart jumped and anger welled up inside of me as I wondered why people won't obey the leash laws. Trying to hide my fright and breathing deeply, I walked across the street. That reminded me that Satan walks "to and fro in the earth, and from walking up and down in it" (Job 1:7). In our lives he is stalking about, looking for ways to frighten us. 1 Peter 5:8 says, "Be vigilant; because your adversary the devil, as a roaring lion, walketh about, seeking whom he may devour."

For some there is little choice about going into Satan's turf— police, firemen, and physicians. But for many of us, we have no business in his territory. John 14:30 calls him "the prince of this world." There are times when we would do best to walk across the street.

a. Most Hollywood films depict a subtle form of humanism, and even though they seem innocent at first, you'd better be aware that little by little your values can change. Your emotions can be changed by a spark that erupts into fires that won't go out.

b. You may need to walk to the other side of your living room and turn off your TV. That tenacious robber of time and shaper of minds dishes out daily diets of "Do your own thing," often at someone else's expense and contrary to God's law.

c. Walk to the nearest trash can and throw away the reading material that turns the healthy emotion of love into lust or jeal-. ousy. Burn books that make sex the be-all and end-all, negating the concepts of companionship, friendships, and male/female relationships.

d. Walk away from so-called friends who would steer you into the path of the world and its system. Satan makes no bones about his authority in Luke 4:6.

e. Don't walk but run past the palm reader's gaudy trailer or any other temptation to dabble in the occult.

Walking isn't always fun or exhilarating. On fresh spring days when the crocuses and tulips lift their noble heads in splendid hues, I could walk forever. In autumn the dazzling yellows, or- anges, and reds of leaves waving goodbye to another year put on a glorious show that entices me to walk. The smell of damp leaves, burning leaves, and the crunch of dry leaves brings flashbacks to years gone by; the nostalgia is at the same time pleasant and sad. Walking gives me time to muse and meditate. I don't even mind walking in the freshly fallen snow. But, after the newness of snow wears dark coveralls for days and bitter cold bites my cheeks, I get bored, and excuses for not walking are obvious. The length of winter and the gray sameness sometimes overwhelms me, and I so long for the new greenness of spring.

So it may be in our walk with the Lord sometimes. Often we can feel His presence, and our hearts are full of springtime so it's easy to sing praises to Him. But there are days, many more than I like to acknowledge, when we must just walk on. Just walk on without feelings, without pats on the back, or even without confirmation that we are walking in the right way. Just walk on. According to 2 Corinthians 5:7, we must walk by faith, not by sight.

Stretching Your Forgetter

People say I'm getting old because I forget so much. The way I look at it, that's not getting older, that's getting better.

a. We can be better company if we forget hurts and don't hold grudges.

b. We can be more stable emotionally if we can forget the highs as well as the lows.

c. We can be better as loving communicators. When our families realize that we won't drag up a past failure and hurt list, they feel free to share their dreams and pain.

d. We can be better servants because we don't rest on our laurels: how many people we've led to Christ, how much we did, or how hard we worked.

Forget yesterday and give today all we have. Try to give 100 percent and then no one is cheated. If we don't get the same in return—forget it!

Sometimes while we are trying to keep our gym clean, we are successful in keeping out fear, jealousy, and greed, but Satan will trick us. He will suggest we meditate on something that is true, that really happened, and the more thinking we do, the more upset or angry we become.

Lest you think I have resorted to boasting, let me share one of my favorite verses and one that I use with every book I autograph:

> I do not consider, brethren, that I have captured and made it my own [yet]; but one thing I do—it is my one aspiration: forgetting what lies behind and straining forward to what lies ahead, I press on toward the goal to win the [supreme and heavenly] prize to which God in Christ Jesus is calling us upward (Phil. 3:13–14, AMPLIFIED).

We're not writing this book because we have arrived at a state of spirituality that makes us superior. On the contrary! We know we haven't arrived; in fact the more we learn, the more we find that we don't know anything. But, like Paul, we can do this one thing, we can *forget*.

You ask, what do you do if:

Sally Sewer is running her mouth again? *Forget it!*

Hubby habit forgot your birthday again? *Forget it!*

Everyone was asked to the luncheon but you? *Forget it!*

Remember that every victory and every sorrow is being used of God to fashion you into the image of His Son.

The more I stretch my forgetter, the more alert my mind becomes to the essentials. The clean, fresh breezes of creativity can move in. Ideas can exercise in a clean gym without the riff-raff.

Running the Race

It is an absolute certainty that I will grow immensely in the emotional *and* spiritual areas of my life by running the race.

I have never won a prize for anything, and if it weren't for the prizes offered by the Judge as He sits in the reviewing stands up there, I feel sure I wouldn't ever win one. But as I view this life for all that it is, I see that it is a race: a. A race against time. b. A race against the enemy. c. A race that supersedes all others.

> Know ye not that they which run in a race run all, but one receiveth the prize? So run, that ye may obtain (1 Cor. 9:24).

We have all heard the story of Paul Revere racing against the clock, crying the message, "The British are coming!" We are not running just for health or even for the prize, but because of the importance of our message. "Holding forth the word of life; that I may rejoice in the day of Christ, that I have not run in vain, neither laboured in vain" (Phil. 2:16).

Again, I remind you we are but vessels carrying a precious cargo, the Lord Jesus Christ. How we carry the Word determines whether or not we have run in vain.

A good runner strips herself of excess weight:

> Wherefore seeing we also are compassed about with so great a cloud of witnesses, let us lay aside every weight, and the sin which doth so easily beset us, and let us run with patience the race that is set before us (Heb. 12:1).

Our Cheering Section

While in high school I was a cheerleader. My "man" was Larry and when he was up for a foul shot, I would get on the sidelines and lead our section in, "Larry, Larry, he's our man. If he can't do it, nobody can!" I often wondered how it would feel to have someone cheering for me. I know now that I do. It's that great cloud of witnesses who have run the race before me and succeeded. These people had faith—they "stuck to" what they knew God wanted them to do through tough tests. They are recorded in the eleventh chapter of Hebrews as the heroes of the faith, and if they made it so can I.

I began to change because I knew Christ wasn't pleased with me. I began sticking with things, whether it was walking, running, or just waiting. Being faithful to what God wants me to do and be has strengthened me tremendously.

The story is told of a village blacksmith who expressed the only fear he had, that of being thrown on the scrap heap. He explained how he tempered steel by heating it, hammering it, and then quickly dashing it into a bucket of cold water. He found out very soon whether it would take tempering or go to pieces in the process. He said if he found that, after one or two tests, it was not going to allow itself to be tempered, he threw it on the scrap heap and sold it for junk.

He likened the tests he used to temper steel to those that were dealt to him by God. He wanted to take the tests to become strong, but he didn't want to go to pieces or refuse to yield to the heat. He knew the danger of being thrown on the scrap heap with the label: Unusable. (See 1 Cor. 9:25–27.)

"If God Said I Could Mount Up With Wings as Eagles, How Come I'm Down Here With These Turkeys?"

This is a humorous question, but it is often true. God tells us to set our affections on the heavenlies, but often we are too involved with the nasty now and now. It is essential that we know God is involved with us personally, and that our walk with Him does not have to be affected by the negative attitudes of others. We have this promise:

> But they that wait upon the Lord shall renew their strength; they shall mount up with wings as eagles; they shall run, and not be weary; and they shall walk, and not faint (Isa. 40:31).

God knows there are times when we can run and times when we can only walk. He also understands that there are times when we can do neither.

A dear friend of mine is bedridden now for the eighth week after injuring her knee. Because she has a disease that weakens her muscles anyway, it is doubly difficult. While she waits in bed, she exercises the muscles she can.

Emotionally, we can be so injured that for a time we don't seem to be able to walk, let alone run. God says that is the time to rest in Him and exercise your emotional muscles another way. In a time when I was injured emotionally, before I could go out and articulate what God was doing in my life, before I could teach, speak, write, or exercise any of those muscles I had to wait to be restored. But while waiting, I began an exercise that helped me more than any other. It is an exercise to renew my mind, and it is still part of my every waking moment.

By nature, I have a negative, pessimistic, melancholy temperament. I see black clouds hovering over everything. When I would wake up, I knew it would be a bad day. If somebody did something nice for me, I would wonder what their hidden motive was. I was critical and picky, and my dark shroud touched everything. Now, transforming that mess has taken some work, but by God's grace, I am doing what Romans 12:1–2 says to do:

> I beseech you therefore, brethren, by the mercies of God, that ye present your bodies a living sacrifice, holy, acceptable unto God which is your reasonable service. And be not conformed to this world; but be ye transformed by the renewing of your mind, that ye may prove what is that good and acceptable and perfect will of God.

For me a renewed mind is the exact opposite of my old mind. Where I "naturally" see gloom and doom, I have had to teach myself to see beauty and goodness. Instead of dwelling on what goes wrong or what I don't have, I have had to learn to look for what is going right and what I do have. Let me give you one example.

I hate cars that are not dependable and break down. And mine always seems to break down when my husband is out of town. I used to be bent out of shape for days after I went through the ordeal of being towed into a garage where I had to relinquish the car to a total stranger and trust that person to get me home.

The first time I applied the renewing principle to that type situation will always stand out in my mind. It takes about forty minutes to get from far south Tampa to north Tampa where we lived; my car broke down in between. Steaming mad after waiting two hours in the July sun for AAA to tow me, I was finally towed to far south Tampa. Not being able to locate a friend to drive me home, I got in a car with a mechanic who was nearly buried in beer cans and cigarette butts. Once home, my nerves raw from forty minutes of the loudest rock music, I worked out my frustrations in the hot yard.

"O.K. God, I'm supposed to thank You for everything. I don't feel like praising, but here goes." With that much obedience I began to see things I could be thankful for:

    a. We *did* have AAA.
    b. The young man did get me home safely.
    c. I *did* find a neighbor who offered to take me to retrieve my car.
    d. I could have had an accident instead of an incident.

Now, I realize that those weren't very lofty, profound thoughts, but they got me started looking for something good in a bad situation.

I don't want you to get the idea that I'm doing the renewing. All I do is agree with God that I need renewing and lift up or yield myself to Him to do it. What differences do I see? Instead of being angry for having a headache *again*, I count the days that I didn't have one. Instead of counting all the dirty clothes to be washed, I thank God for a family healthy enough to dirty them. Instead of grumbling over a two-hour flight that took fifteen because of fogged-in airports, I enjoy the opportunity to get to know strangers and perhaps witness to them.

I have talked to many women over the past few years about suicide, and I'm shocked by so many who have tried it as many as eight times. I shouldn't be so amazed, because if I hadn't gotten a clear picture of myself sitting on a shelf, swinging my legs over a sign that said: "unusable, castaway—not worth the price paid," I would probably have considered doing it again. Instead, I have taken one step at a time until my emotional muscles have become stronger. Oh, the thorny places are still to be gotten through. The heat is sometimes nearly unbearable, and the water threatens to drown me, but God says, in effect, that He doesn't take me through the fire to burn me but to temper and strengthen me. He doesn't take me through deep waters to drown me but to teach me to swim.

> But now thus saith the Lord that created thee . . . Fear not: for I have redeemed thee, I have called thee by thy name; thou art mine. When thou passest through the waters, I will be with thee . . . when thou walkest through the fire, thou shalt not be burned; neither shall the flame kindle upon thee (Isa. 43:1–2).

Just as in a race, one of our most precious commodities is ticking away as I write this. By the time you read it I will barely remember the day I wrote it. We all have the same number of hours in a day but in order to win the race we must make every minute count. Don't try to run while carrying harmful emotions as weights. We must lay them aside.

Use your mind's own built-in "Logic Ladder" to simplify life's daily problems.

When trying to solve a problem, the mind thinks in a set sequence of logical operations. This sequence occurs so quickly that we often don't realize it is happening, but nevertheless, the mind works toward a conclusion in every situation through a series of internal steps. And much as the steps of a ladder are arranged in an orderly fashion to reach the top of a building, so too God has equipped our minds to function along a series of logical steps to reach solutions to the problems of everyday life. These mental steps to effective problem solving can be conceptualized as a "Logic Ladder" with seven sequential steps. In the following pages we will look at each of these steps, and how using them can enable

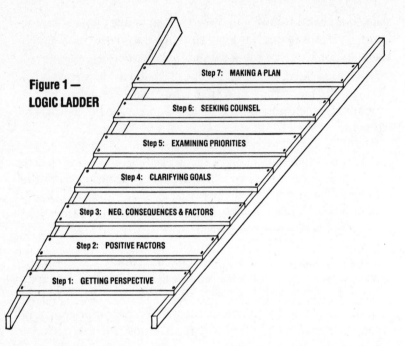

Figure 1 —
LOGIC LADDER

Step 7: MAKING A PLAN

Step 6: SEEKING COUNSEL

Step 5: EXAMINING PRIORITIES

Step 4: CLARIFYING GOALS

Step 3: NEG. CONSEQUENCES & FACTORS

Step 2: POSITIVE FACTORS

Step 1: GETTING PERSPECTIVE

you to think and solve problems more effectively. (See Logic Ladder Figure 1.)

Step 1: *Getting Perspective*

The first step to better thinking is to look at all aspects of a situation without limiting your vision. Many times logical thinking becomes clouded at this very first step because we react instinctively to a situation by impulsively liking or disliking it. Sometimes such instantaneous reactions can be useful because they shield out irrelevant information; but more often, the unwillingness to be broad-minded leaves us enslaved to our own prejudices and preconceived notions. In Matthew 9:16–17 Christ makes the point that we are to have a mental outlook which is flexible like a new wine skin, rather than rigid like an old one. He warns that His trying to put new wine (new truths and new ideas) into old wine skins (our closed minds) will only result in frustration and failure for us. This lack of flexibility can tremendously limit God's opportunity to show us new solutions to tough problems.

Step 2: *Positive Factors*

After having accomplished the first step of deciding to be broadminded and looking at all aspects of a situation, the next step is to consider the positive factors (or influences) resulting from the situation. You might want to take three or four minutes to simply review all the possible positive factors or influences which might have an impact on the situation. Factors such as increased family time or a better standard of living might be positive factors impacting a job change opportunity. Try to tune out any negative thinking at this step; that will come later. Here, at step two, let your mind dig and search for every possible positive factor associated with a situation. Remember, at step one, you made the decision to be open-minded in this process of logic, so don't let something new or unfamiliar inhibit your speculation about its potentially positive aspects. (Note: A helpful technique is to look at the possible outcome of a decision at four different distances in the future: the *immediate* results of the decision, the *short-range* results, the *medium-range* results, and the *long-range* results. The decision which may not appear to have much to offer in the way of immediate results may look very positive in its medium- to long-range results.)

Step 3: *Negative Consequences and Factors*

Once you have accomplished steps 1 and 2, it is time to look at possible negative aspects to the decision. Again, projecting the outcome of a decision into four future distances (immediate, short-range, medium-range, and long-range) will be helpful. Also, don't just look at the surface consequences of a situation, but look at the possible secondary consequences as well. For example, a home may appear to be an excellent buy as it sits in a lush and cool shady valley in the summer, but that same valley may have a history of flooding in the spring.

Step 4: *Clarifying Goals*

"What are my real aims and objectives in this situation?" Many times we find that the goal that we are really hoping to achieve is not necessarily the one to which our decisions are taking us. Sometimes, while we are pursuing one goal we are almost unknowingly led astray by another goal. The intense pursuit of one aim may keep us from reaching another far more important one. For example, if your goal is to raise emotionally sound children, it would be defeating to that goal to become engaged in so many different activities that you scarcely have adequate time to spend with your children.

Step 5: *Examining Priorities*

Once you have clarified the goal you are trying to reach, and before developing a plan of action, you need to take a quick but careful look at just how the decision and goal in question fit into your life priorities. When discussing the proper ordering of priorities, Jesus said in Matthew 6:33 that He would bless us if we would seek first His kingdom (His activities) and His righteousness (His character qualities) in our decisions of life. In Chapter 11 we examined a recommended order of priorities for the Christian.

Step 6: *Seeking Counsel*

The Scripture teaches that it is a mark of wisdom to seek mature counsel when making a decision. "Listen to counsel and accept discipline, that you may be wise the rest of your days" (Prov. 19:20, NASB). In fact, the Scriptures warn us not to regularly make decisions based solely on our own wisdom and understanding. The Lord doesn't want us to be spiritual "Lone Rangers," and He goes so far as to say that when we isolate ourselves we are just being unwise and even selfish (Prov. 18:1). The key to success in this step lies in picking the right counselor(s). We would suggest as a rule of thumb going to at least three different counselors for advice when making a major decision. These counselors should be trustworthy and spiritually wise. Try not to pick individuals who will all approach the decision from the same viewpoint. You are not looking for a counselor who will automatically say what he or she thinks you want to hear, and neither do you want a counselor who will feel automatically compelled to contest the preferences of your heart. A way to increase your benefit from a counseling session with another person is to write down beforehand whatever views you feel the other person is likely to have about your situation. Apart from advice that is clearly a mandate from Scripture, by comparing the counsel you thought they *might* give you before the session with the counsel they actually *did* give you in the session, you will be more apt to separate those comments which were really relevant, personalized, and helpful from those which were automatic and "off the cuff."

Step 7: *Making a Plan*

It has been said that the individual who aims at nothing can be assured of hitting it. The point here is that we should decide upon an adequate plan of action, one that is simple yet will bring us to our desired goal. Of course, there are often complications which require us to modify plans along the way, and therefore, whenever we make a single plan to reach our goal, we must be sure that we have made a second contingency plan as well. The contingency plan is that plan which will be used only if our original plan runs into trouble.

Study Questions

1. Name the steps that lead to a stronghold in your mind.
2. What four steps must be taken to rid ourselves of strongholds?
3. What does 2 Corinthians 10:4–5 teach us about strongholds?
4. How do imaginations become our enemies?
5. Discuss how to use the Word of God as a weapon against Satan.
6. What great exercise does Philippians 3:13 teach?
7. Do you think a negative person can be changed into a positive one? What verse would you use?
8. How can the Logic Ladder help you in your daily life?

PART III

The Spirit

Chapter 13

Introduction to the Spirit

Kissed by the Spirit

The same old fear and morbidity silted into my being as the shroud of darkness settled slowly around our Alabama yard. By day, summer clung to October in 1966, but winter sneaked in by night, hiding the stars and filling me with dread.

Why so hopeless? Why this unnamed malady for so long? I had a wonderful husband who loved me, three healthy, happy children, lived in a new house, drove a new car, and had purchased much of the American dream. At what point, then, had I been disappointed? Why did I dread night? Why did my heart hurt so? It all seemed so silly, and I seemed to be so alone that I didn't bother to communicate my feelings. My hurting heart had suffered for years. It was a mysterious pain that couldn't be healed by human love or acquisitions, but it could be masked by busy daytime activities.

I felt shame for my disappointment when I enjoyed so many blessings. I seemed lost in dark, lonely woods. Loneliness surrounded me in the midst of a loving family and many friends. I couldn't answer the nagging question, "Why am I here?" That was the biggie; why was I here? There had to be more purpose to life than I was experiencing.

There was one difference on this particular night. A pastor of a small, new church had visited me since I was a newcomer to town. He seemed to be able to look right through me and see my emptiness, loneliness, and my longings for someone I hadn't yet met. This quiet, gentle man seemed to exude all that I was missing, and I clung to his every word. George O'Brian said, "Of course you feel lonely because the Word of God says, 'Your iniquities have separated between you and your God, and your sins have hid his face from you' (Isa. 59:2). You see, God made you for a purpose and has a plan for your life. He loves you very much and wants you to be His child."

I momentarily bristled at the mention of sins. I explained that I had been *faithful* to church, *read my Bible*, and *prayed* since I was a small child. I did many kind things for those in need and assumed many responsibilities in my church. I was much better than many I knew.

Pastor O'Brian said he admired those good deeds but that I shouldn't rely on my goodness because according to God's standard, there is none good (Matt. 19:17). He explained that when I measured myself by God's goodness rather than human, I would understand.

What also made this evening different was the little pamphlet the pastor had left behind a few weeks earlier. I read and reread it. I had already learned much of it as a child, but I still couldn't see the point of it all. That was before I understood how God uses His Word to draw us.

Desperate for peace and forgiveness, desperate to fill my empty, futile life, desperate to know Him, I pulled out the dog-eared tract to read for the twentieth time. After my family had long turned in sleep, the struggle was over, and I wanted changing. I felt dead, but it was still painful to read:

There is none righteous, no, not one. For there is no difference: For all have sinned, and come short of the glory of God (Rom. 3:10, 22–23).

"For the wages of sin is death" (Rom. 6:23).

There were many other things in the pamphlet I was trying to understand: God loved me so much that He sent His Son to pay the wages for my sin. God gave His only begotten son, Jesus Christ, as my substitute, who bore my sin and died in my place.

He hath made him to be sin for us, who knew no sin; that we might be made the righteousness of God in him (2 Cor. 5:21).

I saw that when Christ died in my place He shed His precious blood, "For the life of the flesh is in the blood." "Without shedding of blood is no remission" (Heb. 9:22). I saw that He arose from the dead, and because of His resurrection, He could come and live in me if I would ask Him. The tract instructed me to call upon the name of the Lord:

For whosoever shall call upon the name of the Lord shall be saved (Rom. 10:13).

In the tract were these words:

The first prayer for a sinner to pray is given in Luke 18:13, "God be merciful to me a sinner."

Right now, wherever you are, lift your heart to God in prayer. It does not take a long, loud prayer, for God is anxious to save you. Just say: "Oh, God, I am a sinner. I am sorry, I repent, have mercy upon me, and save me for Jesus' sake." Now just take Him at His Word. For whosoever shall call upon the name of the Lord, shall be saved.

Just as simply as I knew how, I prayed those words. Without any outward emotion, inwardly I knew something had happened to me. The dread and fear melted out of me, and peace and joy began building. The knowledge of cleansing overwhelmed me. I sat for a long time in wonder. I was new. "Therefore if any man be in Christ, he is a new creature: old things are passed away; behold, all things are become new" (2 Cor. 5:17).

It was the work of God the Holy Spirit to draw me by the Word of God to Jesus, the Son of God, to quicken deep within me, to awaken my corpse of a spirit. It is simple to hear and believe the facts about Christ, but not so simple to place your complete trust in those facts as the solution to your spiritual dilemma. After months of agony and evidence weighing, it was the simple, childlike act of placing my complete trust in Jesus Christ.

My conversion experience reminds me of the story of the prince who kissed Sleeping Beauty to wake her. The exact moment I turned to Christ as my personal Savior, the Holy Spirit touched me and I "awoke" out of darkness into His Light. This is called "quickening" in the Bible:

> But if the Spirit of him that raised up Jesus from the dead dwell in you, he that raised up Christ from the dead shall also quicken your mortal bodies by his Spirit that dwelleth in you (Rom. 8:11).

I saw myself as free and clean, loved and satisfied, for the first time. It was like a cool drink on a scorching day. I awoke surrounded and infused with peace. That was my spiritual birth, my beginning, on that dark, starless night in October, 1966. That, in fact, was the first time a balanced life was even possible for me.

Malcolm Browne, writing in the *New York Times*, asked a question that wouldn't have been pertinent a few years ago: "Just how much of a person could be replaced by spare parts before turning him into someone else?" The article then listed some of the scientific accomplishments such as the use of ceramics for implanting tooth substitutes and synthetic polymers as heart components and blood vessels.

Astounding advances in medical science have been achieved, but no substitute has been found for that part of a person's nature that is dead toward God. Failing kidneys, livers, and lungs can be replaced by transplantation, and Barney Clark even lived for many weeks with an artificial heart. But a person who is spiritually dead must have a quickening (lifegiving) touch from God. When this takes place, there is no "patching up" with spare parts, but a totally "new creation." For those who have not experienced a new birth, in John 1:12 Christ says, "But as many as received him, to them gave he power to become sons of God, even to them that believe on his name."

If you have never asked Christ to come into your heart through His Spirit as Lord and Savior, you can do it now. Right where you sit, as you are reading this book, He is seeking entry into your heart for the present and for all eternity. (See John 1:12.)

When I asked Christ into my heart, it was at that moment that my earthen vessel received its new contents. Long before I knew about the filling of the Holy Spirit, long before I understood that, I was filled. For the first time I was carrying "this precious treasure." I had found a purpose for my life.

When I finally went to bed, my husband held me as I shared what had happened. He told me that at the age of fifteen, he had done the same thing. While there were many godly qualities about him, he was untaught in the Scriptures. As a couple, we were more one than ever before.

The following Sunday we decided to visit the pastor's small church because of the love he had shown us. We were in for quite a shock because the church met in a small, rather ramshackle house that still possessed a kitchen sink and stove right behind the pulpit. There were something like thirty-five members present on that day, and while they may not have dressed with as much class as some of the people at larger churches, they had more than enough love to share with us. We decided to join the church after I was baptized. But, we soon found out that there is more to living the Christian life than sitting in church. How to live that life became important. Sadly, like so many, we began to sense a "hidden list" of things Christians are and are not supposed to do.

In our newness, we didn't stop to think that in different cultures, countries, or demoninations the list may be different. So, we made our first false assumption about the Christian life.

I had come to Christ as an unbalanced person who had neglected the spiritual side. But as we began a negative course of keeping a list of rules that were not scripturally based, I went all the way to the point of becoming spiritually unbalanced to the other extreme. If you live according to God's Word, without carrying around a self-made do and don't list, you cannot become spiritually unbalanced. But, I began a self-imposed program of neglecting my body and my emotions. I nearly knocked people over in my desire to see them have "what I had." I'm sure I insulted many sincere Christians who were not bound by the set of rules I was trying to live by.

I decided that my lovely clothes were too vain, so I began to make clothes for myself and my daughter—and I don't sew! I have the greatest admiration for anyone who can put a zipper in. I know we began to look like we belonged in *Tobacco Road* as I smiled radiantly and invited my sophisticated friends to receive the same life-changing experience as I had. I could read into their faces a resounding, "No, thank you!"

I believed any far-fetched ideas I heard in just about any kind of service, whether it was giving up our insurance because Jesus would come back before we used it or selling our nice new home and moving into a small, ugly place in the country where we could "farm." We knew as much about farming as I knew about sewing.

No one who knew me before could believe how I looked or lived. Little did I know that I was marring the message I was supposed to be carrying by thinking "godly" was drab and ugly. I hadn't thought about the fact that God didn't make one ugly flower. Even dandelions are not ugly. I was convincing very few to become Christians because of the long list of negatives I was keeping.

In those early days I would rush through breakfast, get the kids ready, meet the school bus, then grab my Bible and slip into the "spiritual" part of my day. After prayer I would get back to housework until I could go back to my prayer closet to be "spiritual."

Much later, I came to understand that if we are walking in the Spirit, everything we do is spiritual. Dishes. Canning. Hanging out clothes. Everything. You don't slip in and out of a spiritual state. The normal Christian life is a moment by moment walking in the Spirit. If that is untrue, we would be wise to enter a convent where we can meditate and pray without outside interruptions. We are created to bring glory to Christ by living day by day according to His Word.

As years went by and we were busy with our ministry of Child Evangelism Fellowship and our family, I began to segregate what I thought was spiritual from the mundane things that had to be done. I constantly felt guilty because I didn't spend enough time in prayer and Bible study, although I did spend at least half an hour in devotional time. Rather than enjoy the freedom in Christ, I tied bundles of burdens around my neck. As the children began entering the teen years and responsibilities became greater, I was recovering from what was diagnosed as a severe bout of multiple sclerosis. Attempting to be mother *and* father while Marvin was out trying to win the world pushed me emotionally out of balance. I introspectively evaluated every thing I did. What was my motive? Had I really "given it my all"? I spent more and more time reading my Bible and praying, but nothing I did seemed holy enough. I became convinced that I was so unworthy that everything I did was in the flesh and thus a failure. Combined with the guilt were hidden anger and fear that turned into full-fledged depression. This course led me to the suicide attempt in 1975. (That story is told in *Dear Mama, Please Don't Die.*)

Easter Sunday I took forty sleeping pills to put to sleep a woman who was gravely ill—body, soul, and spirit. Days later that same woman woke up still ill. But I had to ask myself, "Why did God spare me if I am so worthless?" Was He telling me that living the Christian life His way was different than the way I knew? If I tried so hard and still wasn't spiritual, how would I ever find out what was spiritual?

Calling upon God to cleanse me from the horrible sin I had committed, I lay in my hospital bed cleansed because of His promise in 1 John 1:9. I was too weak to do much reading and praying. I would not be out of the hospital for weeks, so my teaching and other "spiritual" tasks would have to remain undone. Was I to just lie there in the flesh waiting for the time I could be "spiritual" again? Or was I to learn a lesson on true spirituality?

Why is a daisy always a daisy? Because it cooperates with the Creator in being what He made it to be. It glorifies God. George Mueller said in a message he preached in Dublin, Ireland, "Friends, how many objectives do you have in life? Three? Then you have two too many! Two? Then you have one too many! One, and that one *the glory of God*? Then you are like your Master!" Keeping that one goal in mind, we can change the most commonplace things of life into treasures to lay at the Master's feet.

True spirituality on an individual basis is cooperating with God, moment by moment, in becoming what He meant for you to be, thus glorifying Him and being a blessing to Him. When this is so, you will naturally be a blessing to others. Such living eradicates lists of stagnant dos and don'ts and replaces them with conduct guided solely by a desire to apply the Word of God in becoming as much like Christ as possible. This will give you great freedom to blossom under the direction of the Holy Spirit.

Again, let me point you to "this treasure" we have in our earthen vessels (2 Cor. 4:7); the Treasure should be able to shine through. That means we don't do anything that hinders the ultimate purpose of our lives. It is a moment by moment yielding to God for a filling of the Spirit who lives in us, manifesting the fruit of the Spirit and a moment by moment trusting Him.

When I stopped yielding and trusting in order to carry around my burdens by myself, I fell. When I assessed the fall, I saw that my physical vessel was crushed, and the wrong emotions were spilling out. At the same time, I was forced to make an evaluation spiritually. I saw my condition as one of hunger, weakness, nakedness, and uncleanness. I had allowed myself to be contaminated with sins of anger, fear, discouragement, despair, and hopelessness—not much different from when I came to Christ initially. I needed cleansing and a thorough understanding of the blood of Christ and His Word as it applies to staying pure.

My spiritual diet needed a boost found only in devouring God's Word. Just as important as sitting down to meals three times a day was setting up a regular schedule for digesting Scripture. *Not from a legalist list of rules*, but from a hunger that needed feeding.

My spiritual muscles were flabby due to lack of exercise, and like Adam and Eve, I had allowed myself to become spiritually naked, and by faith, I needed to clothe myself.

The message I had conveyed was that Christ was not sufficient, yet Christ is *always* sufficient! It is up to me not to shut off His supply of life-sustaining grace by choosing to believe the lies of Satan. How could I rectify what I had done? How can you?

I had to recognize that all the harmful emotions I discussed in previous chapters led to a deeper spiritual problem. Anger towards life circumstances ultimately leads to anger toward God. We say to ourselves, "After all, He could change things if He so desired; He is God isn't He?" My lack of understanding *true spirituality* led to the following disastrous consequences:

a. Satan gaining a stronghold.
b. Spiritual apathy.
c. A sense of failure and feeling of being put on the shelf spiritually.
d. Fear of getting to the heart of the matter and receiving help.
e. An intense but brittle confidence in legalism. I had busied myself with the rules without getting to know the score-keeper. Like many I got the cart before the horse.

I failed to realize that for the Christian, all of life is sacred; it is to be lived to bring glory to God, through His gift of grace, not our works. Unfortunately, many Christians say, "I don't drink, smoke, dance, or go to movies, and I read three chapters in the Bible a day, pray, work for the church, and that makes me acceptable."

The Christian Life: Sovereignty or Slavery?

As Christians, we have the privilege of choosing how we will live the new life in Jesus which God has given us. The chains by which Satan had bound us so cruelly before salvation are rendered powerless by the blood of Christ. Yet although we are all free, many Christians mistakenly choose to live as if they were still wearing the chains of Satan's bondage from their previous lifestyle. Bondage to old habits, fears, traditions, desires, relationships, needs, thoughts, and weaknesses plague scores and scores of Christians; and yet the Scriptures teach us an alternative. The Scriptures teach us how we can live in a condition of sovereignty (as free sons and daughters of Jesus Christ) rather than in a condition of slavery (in the grip of our own impulses or in the futility of legalism).

The key to living the Christian life in sovereignty rather than struggling along in slavery begins in John 14:6, "Jesus saith unto him, 'I am the *way*, the *truth*, and the *life*: no man cometh unto the Father, but by me'" (emphasis mine). We must first believe that Jesus is the WAY to God, not only for salvation, but also in our daily living. By knowing Christ through studying His Word and praying daily, we are carrying out what God wants us to be doing first and foremost with our lives. Modern Christianity has almost "choked" itself with its seemingly endless projects, rules, plans, schedules, organizational charts, and activities. All of these are emphasized as being means of participating in the goals and worship of the church; and yet, it is knowing and obeying God through our personal relationship with Christ which really pleases God.

Second, we must believe that Christ is the *TRUTH*. In other words, we must develop an absolute confidence in the Word of God. Through personal devotions, group Bible study, and receiving sound doctrinal teaching, we can become fully confident that the Scriptures are a worthy and reliable source of strength and guidance in every situation we face. "All scripture is inspired by God and profitable for teaching, for reproof, for correction, for training in righteousness; that the man of God be adequate, equipped for every good work" (2 Tim. 3:16–17, NASB).

Finally, we must believe that Jesus is the *LIFE*. We must decide within ourselves that knowing, trusting, and following Him is what real balance and fulfillment in life is all about. The world and its system of short-term rewards provides the glittering, raucous, and alluring temptation of an alternative lifestyle. Yet we as Christians must know that to really live is to experience the renewal and satisfaction of a personal relationship with Jesus Christ.

Refusing to be deterred by any confusion in the church or temptation from the world, we can move progressively toward true spirituality and the sovereign liberty which it affords to the Christian. The key is to know and experience Christ as the way, truth, and life of our spirits in our daily living.

Study Questions

1. Share brief testimonies about when you came to know the Lord. How, when and where?
2. What do you believe a person must understand in order to become a Christian?
3. Does becoming a Christian automatically make a person balanced? Discuss.
4. What do you believe is true spirituality?
5. John 14:6 tells us three things we must believe about Jesus Christ. Discuss.

Chapter 14
Cleansing the Spirit

Soap That Works

The Art of Eating Soap

While explaining the cleansing power of the blood of Christ to my Good News Club, I was interrupted by a little five-year-old red-headed girl who said, "If I eat a bar of soap, won't that clean me up inside?" It reminded me of the strange lengths to which some Christians go to avoid the *one way* we've been given by God to really cleanse our spirits.

I explained that the blood of Christ is the soap we need. We don't eat it, but by faith we believe in it to wash us clean spiritually. Just as we can't clean our bodies with soap alone but also need water, I explained that along with the blood of Christ as the soap, we also need the water of the Word. "Now ye are clean through the word which I have spoken unto you" (John 15:3).

Through the Word we see we are dirty with sin, and through the application of that Word with faith in the fact that God applies the blood, we are made clean. "Come now, and let us reason together, saith the Lord: though your sins be as scarlet, they shall be white as snow; though they be red like crimson, they shall be as wool" (Isa. 1:18).

It is as necessary for me to take a trip to the Word of God each day as it is for me to bathe. Even though I may not be able to see the dirt on my skin, I know I am unclean. Spiritually that is harder. Often I begin reading my Bible not necessarily aware of my sin; when I read something like, "A soft answer turneth away wrath," I'm convicted. Once I recognize my sin, all I need do is confess or own up to it; agree with God that I'm guilty and turn away from it. His job is to cleanse. "But if we walk in the light, as he is in the light, we have fellowship one with another, and the blood of Jesus Christ his Son cleanseth us from all sin" (1 John 1:7).

Whatever the pattern we choose in approaching our daily spiritual cleansing, we must be sure to ask for forgiveness under the blood of Jesus Christ (1 John 1:7), and that we ask for guidance in daily living from the Word of God (Ps. 119:105). Unfortunately, Christians seek to renew their relationship with God by many different things, but as we shall see, in this matter of spiritual cleansing, "One soap works, and one soap doesn't."

One Soap Works and One Soap Doesn't

As Christians, we are told in 1 Peter 1:14–16 (NASB):

As obedient children, do not be conformed to the former lusts which were yours in your ignorance, but like the Holy One who called you, be holy yourselves also in all your behavior; because it is written, "You shall be holy, for I am holy."

The same principle is echoed in 1 John 3:3 which tells us to both fix our hope on Him and also to purify ourselves as He is pure. These are challenging words that may at first seem unattainable.

But when we look further at the Scriptures, we see that God does not expect us to be capable of obeying every aspect of the Bible through our own efforts. Instead, He wants us to seek an abiding and continual relationship with Him. Such an abiding relationship with God is then guaranteed to subsequently result in the kind of godly and pure living to which we are called as Christians. To relate to Him is to love Him, and to love Him is to obey Him; therefore, to relate to Him is to obey Him.

If any one loves Me, he will keep My word; and My Father will love him, and We will come to him, and make Our abode with him. He who does not love Me does not keep My words (John 14:23–24, NASB).

Therefore, we see that one of the "secrets" to an abiding relationship with Jesus Christ is not the futile striving to fulfill every particle of the law, but it is rather the maintenance of an open and "confessed" relationship with Jesus Christ. In 1 John 1:9 the Scriptures teach us that, "If we confess our sins, he is faithful and just to forgive us our sins, and to cleanse us from all unrighteousness."

God is more than willing to engage in an honest and unobstructed relationship with each of His children; but in order for that relationship to exist, each of us must maintain our spirits in a continually cleansed state. This "cleansing" of the spirit involves the continual confession and reconciliation of our lives with the Lord. There are two ways to go about this process of daily "cleansing" our spirits and renewing an open relationship with the Lord. As always in the Scriptures, there is the right way which brings fulfillment and satisfaction, and there is the wrong way which leads to frustration and discouragement. The right way of cleansing the spirit is referred to as the "Soap That Works," and the wrong way of cleansing the spirit is alternately referred to as "Soap That Doesn't Work." In the two columns below we will compare the outcome of these two different attempts to maintain an open and productive daily relationship with the Lord.

Cleansing the spirit with: The Soap That Works	Cleansing the spirit with: The Soap That Doesn't Work
1. Daily cleansing is based on the scriptural "law of liberty," which simply states that acceptability to God is not based on righteous deeds, but on continual fellowship with Christ. In a sense, we are inside the "covering" of Christ's righteousness, having liberty to follow the Holy Spirit and to approach God honestly, confidently, and humbly with our needs and repentance. As Christians we are no longer related to God as aliens, and we do not come under judgment of biblical dos and don'ts. We are free to begin conforming our lives to Christ, which results in the "byproduct," righteous living.	1. Attempting to clean the Spirit with the "soap that doesn't work" is based on attempting to live consistent with the teachings of biblical law by our own initiative and strength. Although few would admit to this philosophy, vast numbers of believers daily undertake to live the Christian life through the keeping of an internally developed system of rules and regulations. These standards of behavior and conduct have become for them a "law" which not only defeats them, but greatly limits their ability to fellowship openly with God.
2. To know God by continually abiding in Him is a Christian's chief goal. This is accomplished by daily cleansing. She does not lower herself to judging other Christians. She maintains her position as a	2. Judging the lifestyles of fellow Christians and unsaved individuals alike is often characteristic of this Christian. The focus of their life is on maintaining a set standard of rules. They violate God's com-

living branch on the "vine" of Christ. Christ tells us in John 15:4–5 to "abide in me."

3. The lives of these Christians are characterized by the encouragement which they express to other Christians. They are a constant source of support and exhortation to their weary brothers and sisters. Because they understand the abundance of grace required to forgive them of their sins, they are willing to extend forgiveness to fellow Christians. They are not afraid to reprove or rebuke, but they do so with great patience and are always careful to share the motives and reasons behind their correction (2 Tim. 4:2).

4. Their objective is to effectively infiltrate the fellowship of other Christians, as well as to infiltrate groups of non-Christians. They understand that to fulfill Matthew 5 as both "the salt of the earth" and "the light of the world," they must invade the world's

mand in Romans 14:4 about judging.

3. These Christians are often too busy with programs and "religious" undertakings to have time to meet the real needs of people. Because they have difficulty understanding the nature of real forgiveness in the God-man relationship, they are likewise insensitive to the more fragile needs of their fellow Christians. Hurrying about in pursuit of a hundred and one peripheral items to the cause of Christ, they miss the very heartbeat of Jesus' ministry, which was developing personal relationships with individuals and sharing how to know God.

4. These Christians' lives are often characterized by an attempt to separate from those members of the church or those members of the world who they deem to be "less than acceptable." They feel that standing apart from the common comings and go-

system. They seek to practice Paul's instructions to be "in the world but not of the world." They do not separate themselves from the world any more than Christ separated Himself from the world.

5. These Christians experience refreshment due to the continual renewing of their relationship with God. They tend to finish well in the Christian faith. The Apostle Paul had instructed his young disciple, Timothy, in the specifics of maintaining a vitally dynamic relationship with Christ. Thus, he could be confident in one of his final challenges to Timothy, "Fight the good fight of

ings of those "less righteous" members of Christianity, they will be set apart as "beacons of holiness." In fact, they have succeeded only in manufacturing in themselves a twentieth century Christian model of the Jewish Pharisee. Because of the internally corrupting nature of this legalism, they become a walking religious facade. Jesus referred to such a lifestyle as being like a white-washed tomb, filled with decay on the inside but glistening white on the outside (Matt. 23:27).

5. These Christians attempt to maintain consistency in the Christian faith for a duration of many years, much in the way a young swimmer may attempt to hold his breath underwater for the duration of an afternoon. Initially it may seem easy; later it becomes uncomfortable; eventually it becomes agonizing; and finally, there is an explosive release of the stale air within the lungs and a gasping for some new and

faith; take hold of the eternal life to which you were called, and you made the good confession in the presence of many witnesses" (1 Tim. 6:12, NASB). In his last letter to Timothy, Paul was able to confirm that he himself had persevered to the end of his life without "burning out." In his words, "I have fought the good fight, I have finished the course, I have kept the faith" (2 Tim. 4:7).

fresh air. In much the same way, the legalistic Christian may be able to manage shallow heart-to-heart communications with God that may go for some time. He appears to be in control of his spiritual life, only to "explode" and depart from the faith later in life. The sides of the spiritual road which the legalists travel are littered with the emotional carcasses of Christians who have attempted to frame for themselves a morally self-righteous lifestyle, only to have that lifestyle eventually collapse of its own weight.

I find that a simple and yet effective way to assure myself I am covering the basic requirements of a daily spiritual renewal in my relationship with the Lord is to check myself against these five "Rs" of a relationship with God:

Regularity. Am I generally consistent in seeking quality prayer time alone with the Lord for confession, praise, and personal requests?

Real Transparency. Am I absolutely open with the Lord about my attitude, motivation, desire, or behavior? (To try to disguise anything from His searing gaze is totally futile anyway, so we might as well go ahead and tell Him the whole truth.)

Repentance. Am I not only willing to be sorry over a given sin, but am I willing to change my behavior? Real repentance involves both.

Response to the Word. Am I "digging deeper" in the Bible for a better understanding of the nature of God and for clearer guidelines for daily living?

Responsibility. Do I have someone to whom I have made myself responsible for consistency in these matters? The Scriptures teach that "two are stronger than one." It is a tremendous benefit to have someone with whom we can pray, share commitments we've made to the Lord, share promises we've received from the Word, and to whom we can be responsible for maintaining regularity in our time with Him.

Forgiveness Paves the Way

We have contrasted Christians who live in a continual state of confession and renewal with God with Christians who attempt to maintain God's acceptance by the strident and hopeless pursuit of a legalistic moral code. However, another obstacle to the proper cleansing of the spirit which can affect both of these groups, has to do with the necessity of forgiving *others* before we can enter into a genuine relationship of forgiveness with the Lord. In fact, Christ states in Matthew 5:23–24 that if we come before the Lord with an ongoing offense in our heart toward another person, we must first go and settle that offense before we try to continue in our prayers. In essence, chronic bitterness in the heart of a Christian can extinguish the quality of our prayer life and thus hamper our ability to "cleanse" our spirits properly through repentance. The following four questions focus on interpersonal relationships in areas we should examine to see if we are pleasing God with the quality of forgiveness we are demonstrating through our lives.

1. When we are offended, do we often retaliate rather than forgive? What does the Bible say about this?
   A. Leviticus 19:18: _____
   B. Proverbs 20:22: _____
   C. Proverbs 24:29: _____

   D. Romans 12:17: _____

   E. 1 Peter 3:9: _____

2. What should be our proper response when we are offended?

   A. Matthew 5:38–48: _____

   B. Ephesians 4:32: _____

   C. Colossians 3:13: _____

3. What crucial role does interpersonal forgiveness play in the prayer life of the believer?

   A. Mark 11:23–26: _____

   B. Matthew 18:23–25: _____

4. How is Jesus Christ our example of forgiveness?

   A. Colossians 2:13–14: _____

   B. Luke 23:34: _____

Study Questions

1. What two elements are necessary for our cleansing in the spiritual realm? Give references.
2. What does 1 John 1:9 teach us about daily sins?
3. Discuss the difference between slavery to legalism and liberty in Christ.
4. What are the five "R's" of a relationship with God?

Chapter 15
Feeding the Spirit

Devotions and the Word of God

Every day, someone competes for our allegiance. In our modern Western society, advertisers and media manipulators of every kind are paid literally billions of dollars to sway the decisions we make in virtually every area of life. Although the intensity of this barrage is certainly greater today than in generations past, the principle is exactly the same one that man wrestled with in Bible times. That principle is simply this: the thoughts which consistently occupy your mind each day will, in time, become characteristics of your life. Thus, the importance of knowing the Word of God is an indispensable foundation to the Christian's daily life. Concerning this matter, God gave His people explicit instructions:

And you shall love the Lord your God with all your heart and with all your soul and with all your might. And these words, which I am commanding you today, shall be on your heart; and you shall teach them diligently to your sons and shall talk of them when you sit in your

house and when you walk by the way and when you lie down and when
you rise up (Deut. 6:5–7, NASB).

Great men in the Bible have always been marked by one common quality: they sought God personally through daily meditation
on His Words. David understood well the concept that only
through a significant daily relationship with God through His
Word could an individual maintain freshness in the God-man
relationship. The writers of the New Testament echo the same
message. "Let the word of Christ richly dwell within you" (Col.
3:16). "Be diligent to present yourself approved to God as a workman who does not need to be ashamed, handling accurately the
word of truth" (2 Timothy 2:15, NASB).

In the pages that follow, we will focus on two groups of Bible
characters. One group maintained a vital relationship with God,
the LEARNERS, while the other group lost their personal relationship with God and subsequently found their lives collapsing in
tragedy, the BURNERS.

The Learners (Men who maintained a consistent relationship
with God.)

Moses, the man who learned to listen to God.

A study of the life of Moses is in one sense a study of a man who
went through a transition. Although Moses' life was always
marked by zeal and intensity, early in his life it was also marked by
insensitivity to the purposes of God. In fact, the early mistakes that
led to his exile from Egypt came from his unwillingness to listen
and wait on the plans of God. Instead, he took matters into his own
hands and eventually murdered an Egyptian soldier. When God
appeared to Moses some forty years later with plans for the deliv-
erance of Israel from bondage in Egypt, again it was Moses who

had difficulty really listening to what God had to say. Moses repeatedly questioned if God's words of promise and power were
truly meant for his ears, and he doubted that Pharaoh would be
willing to listen to what he had to say (Exod. 6:12–13). Yet the
beautiful miracle of Moses' life was that he continued to relate to
God through a bond a friendship. By the thirty-third chapter of
Exodus, we see Moses now listening very intently to the Lord, just
as a man would listen carefully to the words of his best and most
cherished friend.

> And it came about, whenever Moses entered the tent, the pillar of
> cloud would descend and stand at the entrance of the tent; and the
> Lord would speak with Moses. Thus the Lord used to speak to Moses
> face to face, just as a man speaks to his friend. When Moses returned to
> the camp, his servant Joshua, the son of Nun, a young man, would not
> depart from the tent (Exod. 33:9, 11, NASB).

Here we see that not only had Moses developed an intimate
relationship with God characterized by love and obedience, but
this relationship was also beginning to affect his young teenage
"son" in the faith, Joshua. Many times, mothers of teenagers will
ask me how they can have an impact on their adolescent son or
daughter. Their child is going through that difficult time of life
which marks the transition from childhood to adulthood, the teenage years. As we all know, it is not a time of life when young people
are particularly influenced by our best logical arguments or our
most well-intentioned "sermons," but they do observe us very
intently. They are not so much listening to what we say as they are
observing what we live by. They watch what influences us, and
they know where we get our ideas and information about life.
There is no more potent influence on a teenager's mind than
seeing Mom willingly listen to God through consistent daily devotions that then lead to Christlike living. Teenagers are geniuses at
picking apart inconsistency and hypocrisy, and yet they are very,
very vulnerable to the influences of adult examples. From the
Hollywood advertising executives to the masterminds of modern

cults, it is well known that teenagers are impressed by the commitment of others to a cause. The "cause" that our teenager sees demonstrated by us in our homes should be our dedication to a personal relationship with Jesus Christ. Consistent daily devotions in the Word are the place to begin.

David, a man learning to obey.

The life of David is something of a paradox. There are few men in the Bible who so touched the heart of God. In fact, concerning David, the Scriptures say, "I have found David the son of Jesse, a man after mine own heart, which shall fulfill all my will" (Acts 13:22b). And yet, David was a man who committed some terrible sins, including adultery and murder. These occurred when he wandered away from his commitment to the Lord. What can we learn then from David's life? David was a man who possibly above anyone else in history knew how to admit his mistakes to the Lord and return to a position of fellowship. He was a man who spent much of his life learning to confess and obey. The secret to the continual quality of David's relationship with God, even in the midst of tragically sinful behavior, lies in five principles which he practiced in renewing his relationship with the Lord.

Principle #1 David never reached the point where he was unwilling to come to the Lord with his sins (Ps. 90:8; 139:7).

Principle #2 David was willing to admit that the mistakes that he made were not caused by anyone else; he took responsibility for his own actions (Psalm 51:4).

Principle #3 David was willing to ask God for forgiveness. Sometimes, one of the biggest barriers to restoring a broken relationship with the Lord is an unwillingness to simply ask God to take us back into His fellowship. We can become blinded by our own stubborn pride and wither spiritually because of it. In Psalm 51:2 David asks the Lord: "Wash me thoroughly from mine iniquity, and cleanse me from my sin."

Principle #4 After receiving God's forgiveness for his sins, David was willing to be taught a new way of behavior which was more pleasing to God (Psalm 32:8).

Principle #5 David maintained the belief that God would continually be willing to restore the quality of their former relationship. David continually hoped in the Lord and trusted that God would renew him and restore the joy of their relationship (Ps. 51:10–12).

In spite of some major errors which he made during his lifetime, David remained precious to God because he never quit learning how to repent and draw near again to God. I think David's lifetime verse might well have been Psalm 31:23–24.

Oh love the Lord, all ye his saints: for the Lord preserveth the faithful, and plentifully rewardeth the proud doer. Be of good courage, and he shall strengthen your heart, all ye that hope in the Lord.

Daniel, a man who learned the cost of commitment.

We have seen that Moses was a man who learned to listen to God, and David was a man who learned to confess and obey God. Daniel, however, was a man who grew close to God through learning the cost of his commitment to the Lord. Because of his commitment to maintain a right relationship with God, Daniel's life was continually in jeopardy. In the sixth chapter of Daniel, King Darius threw Daniel into a den of lions because Daniel refused to stop praying and giving thanks to God, a devotional program which he practiced three times a day. Here we see the prophet almost losing his life because he will not stop worshiping the Lord. The principle of commitment to a relationship with God in the face of perilous circumstances is one which sustained Daniel throughout his lifetime. Daniel committed himself to a relationship with God and paid the price. The result was a godly life and a biblical example that we can cherish and imitate.

The Burners (Men who found tragedy because they lost their personal relationship with God.)

Asa, a man who burned out.

In the Old Testament, King Asa of Judah was the son of Abijah. King David was dead and it was a fearful time of continual war in which the northern tribes of Israel were in armed conflict with the southern tribes of Judah. Abijah had apparently been a godly man and a good father to his son Asa, and Asa began his reign as king of Judah in an upright fashion. Indeed, he pleased the Lord in his early days as a monarch. "And Asa did that which was good and right in the eyes of the Lord his God" (2 Chron. 14:2).

Asa not only carried through on the good beginnings his father had made, but he listened to the wise words of the prophet Azariah and became a reformer who led his people into a deeper commitment to the Lord.

Yet King Asa had received a firm warning from the prophet early in his reign which stated:

> Here ye me, Asa, and all Judah and Benjamin; The Lord is with you, while ye be with him; and if ye seek him, he will be found of you; but if you forsake him, he will forsake you (2 Chron. 15:2).

Asa had maintained a kingdom of peace for thirty-five years without any major threats to the survival of the nation Judah. But in the thirty-sixth year of his reign, Baasha the King of Israel decided to make war against King Asa. Apparently, over the long years of peace Asa had allowed his relationship of dependency on God to smolder and "burn out." During the years of peace when he should have been deepening his relationship with God, he instead was sliding into complacency. At the time of crisis when challenged by the armies of Israel's King Baasha, he looked to the pagan armies of Syria for assistance instead of looking to the God who had supported him so faithfully in the past. When the prophet Hanani approached King Asa and confronted him with this inconsistency, rather than repenting and seeking the Lord, King Asa became furious and threw the prophet in prison. (King Asa even oppressed those few citizens remaining who agreed with the prophet Hanani.) Three years later King Asa became desperately ill. Yet he would not seek God but instead turned to the "witch doctors" of his court for assistance. The result was that Asa suffered for two years and then died in the forty-first year of his reign. A young man who had started out with zeal and a clear appreciation for the need to depend on God had "burned out" in the later years of his life. He had forgotten the necessity of renewing a continual relationship with God, and had as a result been unable to "finish the race of life" with dignity and honor.

Uzziah, a man burned up by pride.

We saw that King Asa was a man who burned out through years of not keeping his relationship with the Lord fresh and alive. King Uzziah, on the other hand, was a young king of Judah who fell in his relationship with the Lord because of pride. King Uzziah came to the throne of Judah when he was but sixteen years of age and quickly earned a reputation as a military genius. When at peace, he distinguished himself as an inventor, an agricultural reformer, and a king close to the people. As long as he was young and insecure, he sought the Lord eagerly and God undertook to prosper him marvelously. "And as long as he sought the Lord, God made him to prosper" (2 Chron. 26:5b). But a dreadful thing happened as King Uzziah became strong; in 2 Chronicles 26:16, we see that he took three liberties with his relationship with God which placed a permanent separation between him and the Lord.

First, he began to behave corruptly; second, he began to be unfaithful in his allegiance to the Lord as his God; and third, he blasphemed the Lord by breaking God's rules for the temple. The result was that God used the physical disease of leprosy to crush him, and Uzziah suffered from the disease the rest of his life. He had to live in isolation because of this dreadfully contagious illness. His life had essentially been "burned up" by a pride which had led him to repudiate his relationship with God.

Saul, a man who burned away with madness.

King Saul of Israel was not a man who "burned out" in his relationship to God over the years or a man who "burned up" with pride, but he was a man who throughout his life seemed prone to taking shortcuts in finding the solutions to the problems of his life. He sought shortcuts rather than God, and eventually, he lost everything. Ironically, even his selection as king came about as a result of Israel's desire to take a "shortcut" to prosperity rather than wait on God.

Saul's weaknesses soon began to surface, and his tendency to take shortcuts became evident. In 1 Samuel 13, Saul took it upon himself to offer a burnt offering to the Lord when the prophet Samuel was not available. Saul knew that this was something strictly forbidden by the Lord, but because he noticed the people were losing interest in the battle, he took this shortcut as a means of trying to encourage them. Samuel rebuked him sternly,

> You have acted foolishly; you have not kept the commandment of the Lord your God, which He commanded you, for now the Lord would have established your kingdom over Israel forever. But now your kingdom shall not endure (1 Sam. 13:13–14a, NASB).

Several more times in his reign King Saul took shortcuts "around" the will of God, always with disastrous consequences. In fact, God eventually "regretted that He had made Saul king over Israel" (1 Sam. 15:35). By the time of his death, Saul had become so prone to grasping at shortcut solutions to difficult problems, that he had actually turned to sorcery and consulting with mediums (witches) for advice. He had been a man with tremendous opportunities, yet he "burned away" through a persistent unwillingness to avidly seek the Lord and avoid the temptation of shortcut answers to life's problems.

In the previous pages we have outlined both the benefits of maintaining a daily devotional relationship with Jesus Christ and the dangers of letting such a relationship grow cold and deteriorate. The following is a simple seven step outline for a devotional time. We recommend having a devotional time with the Lord at least every other day. The time commitment is roughly 30 minutes, but the benefits are eternal. First, you will need a Bible, one which you can readily read and understand. We would recommend that you avoid paraphrases of the Bible since they are not actual translations of the original languages of the Scriptures. We would also recommend that you avoid translations which are difficult for you to understand. Your pastor or a mature Christian friend will probably be able to advise you as to a good translation for your use. Second, you'll need a notebook in which you can keep your devotions from day to day. A spiral notebook or three-ring loose leaf notebook both work well for this purpose. You can either copy the seven steps of this daily devotional plan (see the following page) into your notebook for each day's use, or you may photocopy the Seven-Step Daily Devotional Plan as many times as you need.

The Devotional Plan starts with you selecting a study passage. These are simply the verses which you have selected for the day's devotions. About seven to twelve verses is a reasonable size for your day's study passage. Your study passage can come from anywhere in the Scriptures, but we recommend for openers that you take one of the books in the New Testament and go through it chapter by chapter, taking it in seven to twelve verse "chunks."

Study passage: _____
Date: _____

Seven-Step Daily Devotional Plan

1. Slowly and thoughtfully read over the study passage for today.
2. Select a key verse which you want to focus on, and write it out.

3. Do you see a command, warning, or specific principle in this verse?

| Now think personally: |

4. How does my life compare with the truth of this Scripture?

5. Based on the above, what specifically do I need to start, stop, or continue doing in my daily living?

6. Do I have a Scripture promise? If so, enter it here:

7. Three of my prayer requests for myself and others are:
   1) _____
   2) _____
   3) _____

Study Questions

1. Do you agree that the thoughts which consistently occupy your mind each day will in time become characteristics of your life?
2. What were the five principles David followed in renewing his relationship with God?
3. Which Bible character grew close to God through learning the cost of commitment to the Lord?
4. How did King Asa "burn out" in his relationship with the Lord in his later years?
5. Which Bible character burned out because of pride?
6. What happens when we take shortcuts in finding solutions to life's problems rather than seek God?
7. Which Bible character did this?

Chapter 16
Exercising the Spirit

A Powerful Prayer Life

I suppose there are few subjects in the Christian life that have received as much attention on the printed page as prayer. The subject of prayer has been approached from every conceivable perspective, and yet there is one key element which is central to every discourse on the matter. Regardless of various superficial differences, there is one key issue which is the real common denominator in every examination of prayer. It is the issue of *power* in praying. Power in praying is not and can never be an object of pursuit, but it is the byproduct of consistent and intimate communication with God. It is power in prayer, or the lack of it, that is the primary determinant of whether a Christian develops a habit of daily regularity and richness in prayer, or instead slides into a discouraged, erratic pattern of praying. As a statement to summarize life, Shakespeare wrote, "To be or not to be, that is the question." For the Christian, that statement may well be, "To pray with power, or not to pray with power, that is the question."

In the few pages that follow, using the Lord's prayer as a model, we will take a look at one particular method by which we can develop a power-producing prayer life.

When the matter of an effective prayer life came up, Jesus did not speak in generalities or lofty platitudes. He was direct and to the point in this matter, as He was in all His instructions to the disciples. In Matthew 6:6–13 eight steps are recorded which the devout Christian must take in order to initiate a powerful prayer life. These eight steps can transport the willing Christian from God's outer courtyard to His inner throne room wherein truly miraculous things can be accomplished.

Step 1. *Unclouding the Issue* (Matt. 6:6–8)

Christ's first order of business in this matter of prayer was to make the point that prayer is not a monologue carried out for the benefit of religious spectators, but rather a heart-felt dialogue transpiring between God and man within the inner spirit of a person. In Christ's time, much as in our current society, the practice of formal religion was a quite socially acceptable pastime. In America today, very few individuals who depend on public support for their livelihood can afford to be thought of as "anti-religious" or irreverent in their dealings with the organized church. The precedent has been set, and well-perpetuated through the ecclesiastical ranks of American society that "prayer for show" is a highly reputable and often self-serving activity. For example, most major public gatherings will open with some lofty attempt to invoke the blessings of God. This is a fine practice, but unfortunately these pious and often beautiful monologues have over time been accepted more as the rule for effective praying than the exception. Christ taught just the opposite. He taught that prayer was not some beautifully fashioned monologue designed to lift the hearts of men, but rather a heart-searching dialogue be-tween a sweat-drenched Christian and his God, seeking to restore and deepen their personal relationship. After warning sternly

against hypocritical prayers rendered only for the benefit of
onlookers, Christ then points the way to real personal communication with God in verses seven and eight of Matthew chapter
six. Here, He states that we are not to use meaningless repetition
such as rote prayers or pious doxologies. Instead, we are to enter
into honest communication with God. It is well-known that the
"backbone" of effective two-way communication is the proper use
of questions. Questions are useful in searching the motives and
intentions of our own hearts. Questions are likewise useful in
gaining an understanding of God by petitioning His response to
the needs of our own lives. The first step of the eight steps to power
in praying is therefore unclouding the issue of real communication. In this step we are to approach God on a regular basis with all
honesty, expecting to meet Him in bi-directional communication. This step is the beginning point of the Prayer Diamond
which we have taken from Matthew 6:6–13 (see p. 198).

Step 2. *Unveiling Before God* (Matt. 6:9)

The second step in the eight-step Prayer Diamond is the unveiling of our own nature and our ways, of God's nature and His ways.
James 4:8–10 instructs us regarding the seriousness with which we
are to approach God in an attitude of worship. We are told that if
we will draw near to Him, He will draw near to us. We are also told
that we are to draw near in a position of reverence and confession,
being willing to humble ourselves in His presence so that He may
exalt (uplift) us. This exalting (or uplifting) means that we will be
promoted to a position of understanding. Looking within ourselves, examining our own nature and ways, and then comparing
honestly what we find with the nature and ways of God puts us in a
position of true openness with Him. Seeing both the majestic
power of the God who rules the heavens and His absolute holiness
and perfection is the beginning of true worship. Christ Himself
prepared His heart to worship the absolute deity of God the Father
with the following phrase, "Our Father who art in heaven, hal-
lowed be Thy name" (Matt. 6:9, NASB).

In meditating on the true nature of God and comparing it with our own inner nature, we are in effect unveiling and placing ourselves in a position of absolute transparency. The Apostle Paul explains the process in 2 Corinthians 3:18 as follows:

> But we all, with unveiled face beholding as in a mirror the glory of the Lord, are being transformed into the same image from glory to glory, just as from the Lord, the Spirit.

The Apostle Paul was trying to make clear to the church at Corinth that it was only through an unveiled, totally transparent comparison of our human nature with the absolute holiness of God that we could begin to be transformed into the image of Jesus Christ. The purpose of prayer is to develop communication which transforms the believer into the image of Jesus Christ. The absolute unveiling of every known aspect of our personality before God, coupled with a parallel investigation of the deeper parts of His nature constitutes that very necessary step of personal "unveiling." The four groups of verses below are selected for use in meditating on a specific aspect of the God-man relationship. We would suggest that at the beginning of your prayer time with the Lord, you open yourself totally to the searching power of His Holy Spirit. Allow your mind to meditate on:

God's Nature (Ps. 84:11–12; Ps. 89:13–15).
Our Nature and Needs (Ps. 139:23–24; Jer. 17:7–9).
God's Ways (1 Sam. 16:7; 2 Chron. 16:9; Ps. 103:10–14).
Our Ways (Rom. 3:10–12; James 4:7–10; James 1:21–22).

Step 3. *Unconditional Surrender* (Matt. 6:10)

The third step is the renewing of an absolute lordship decision. It goes without saying that until we are willing to give God "free title" to every area of our life, we can really go no deeper with Him in developing a powerful prayer life. In Psalm 27:4 David said that the single thing he sought from the Lord was to have an attitude of total submission to God's every will for his life. David was also wise enough to know that if he would do this, he would dwell in constant fellowship with God throughout his life. To David, no price was too high to pay for that quality of relationship with the living God. In Matthew 6:10, Christ says that we must be willing to allow God to both develop His kingdom *within* us (character qualities marked by faith and honesty) and His will *through* us (a lifestyle of righteousness and commitment). In going through the steps of the "Prayer Diamond" we see that Step 2 is the unveiling of ourselves beside the standard of Jesus Christ's life. Step 2 is one of total capitulation to the sovereignty of God in our lives. Admittedly, we may not know the full content of many areas of our own lives, and therefore we won't always know exactly what we are giving God free title to. God certainly understands this, and will not confront us all at once with too many problems in our lives. Yet, for Him to work any further, He must have our permission to proceed at will into any area which the Spirit may expose. His divine correction and spiritual healing cannot be limited by us to certain "comfortable" areas of our life if we expect to proceed with developing a powerful prayer life. We are called by Christ Himself to deed over our lives in total to the sovereignty of God. The Apostle Paul stated in 1 Corinthians 6:19–20 that we are not our own, but rather have been bought with a price that we may glorify God. If we want our life to be *bold* with His power, then it first must be *sold* to His preeminence.

Step 4. *Understanding the Source* (Matt. 6:11)

Once we have done an honest job of unveiling our life before God and have given Him free license to examine, expose, and constructively change any area which He sees fit, then the process of true understanding can begin. Use James 1:16–17 (NASB) as a focus for meditation,

> Do not be deceived, my beloved brethren. Every good thing bestowed and every perfect gift is from above, coming down from the Father of lights, with whom there is no variation, or shifting shadow.

Use the following two steps to put yourself in touch with understanding the real source of your "daily bread."

1. I am grateful for _____

   _____

2. From life I am learning that _____

   _____

Step 5. *Understanding the Needs and "Debts" of My Life* (Matt. 6:12)

Not only do we need to recognize God as the source of all life itself, but we also need to understand the real nature of our dependence upon Him. Expressing our needs to Him is something we must learn to do with openness and confidence. In Hebrews 4:16 (NASB) the Scriptures teach us, "Let us therefore draw near with confidence to the throne of grace, that we may receive mercy and may find grace to help in time of need."

We would recommend Jeremiah 31:9 as a verse to meditate upon concerning God's love for us as His people and His desire that we seek Him much as a loving Father. Having meditated upon that verse, complete the following two statements:

1. Lord, forgive me for _____

   _____

2. Lord, help me to _____

   _____

Step 6. *Uncovering the Negative Trends of My Life* (Matthew 6:13a)

All of our lives are marked by certain negative trends or "temptations" that we manage to stumble into either consciously or unconsciously. Although God is not the author of temptations which fall upon us (James 1:13), He can help guide us around

temptations which would otherwise entangle our lives. The pre-
requisite to such guidance is a willingness on our part to examine
all the trends which characterize our lifestyles, especially searching for the negative trends. Psalm 90:12 is a verse where Moses
asked God for wisdom in examining (or numbering) the day-to-day
details of his life. In Psalm 91:2–3 David recognizes that it is God
who enables us to escape the snares of daily living, and in Psalm
91:5–8 we find the beautiful promises of God concerning protection of us both by day and night. After meditating on these verses,
completing the following two statements may help you uncover
certain of the trends or "temptations" which may be seeking to
snare you.

1. I often _____

2. Lord, please don't let me _____

Step 7. *Uncovering His Truth* (Matt. 6:13b)

After real understanding has come concerning God as the
source of all good gifts, and after an uncovering of some of the
ongoing trends of our lives, the next step in the process of powerful
praying is to uncover God's deeper truths in the Scriptures. It is
always to be the Word which we return to as a wellspring in time of
spiritual drought.

> Therefore I love thy commandments above gold; yea, above fine
> gold. Therefore I esteem all thy precepts concerning all things to be
> right; and I hate every false way. The entrance of thy words giveth light;
> it giveth understanding unto the simple (Psalm 119:127–28, 130).

Those verses state in simple, yet beautiful fashion the incredible
practical value that God's Word has for daily living. Psalm
119:162–63 and 175–76 (NASB) state the Psalmist's great joy at
finding necessary answers in Scripture to the dilemmas of his life.

I rejoice at Thy word, as one who finds great spoil. I hate and despise falsehood, but I love Thy law. Let my soul live that it may praise Thee, and let thine ordinances help me. I have gone astray like a lost sheep; seek Thy servant, for I do not forget Thy commandments.

While meditating on those verses, uncover Scriptural truths as His way to "deliver us from evil" through the following questions about your most recent Bible reading:

1. Lord, in Your Word You have told me _____

_____

2. Lord, teach me how to _____

_____

Step 8. *Unleashing the Power of God* (Matt. 6:13c)

The last of the Prayer Diamond's eight steps to powerful praying involves making ourselves vessels through which God can unleash His power to accomplish His will on earth. In Matthew 6:13c, the Scriptures are clear in pointing out that the Kingdom, the power necessary to bring it about, and the glory for bringing it about all belong to God. We have the privilege of being His willing assistants in this process. In order to be a part of this magnificent undertaking, we must be honest enough to ask God questions for which we have not been able to find answers. Jeremiah 33:3 (NASB) beckons us to honestly ask God to enlighten us in areas where we feel truly confused. "Call to Me and I will answer you, and I will tell you great and mighty things, which you do not know."

In this last stage of unleashing God's power, He also wants us to be willing to obey Him without reservation. We must remember Christ's stern rebuke of Peter in Matthew 16:23 when He warned Peter that he was thwarting the purposes of God because he was setting his mind not on God's interests but on man's. We must be willing to set our eyes firmly on God's principles in Scripture and their application for our lives and then carry these out with determination. In Psalm 119:112–113 (NASB) David states:

I have inclined my heart to perform thy statutes Forever, even to the end. I hate those who are doubleminded, but I love Thy law.

Meditate upon asking God for understanding, and with willingness to obey Him implicitly, complete the following:

Lord, I am willing to obey your Word by doing the following:

_____

_____

The previous eight steps which make up the Prayer Diamond are merely a way of organizing the powerful prayer principles which Christ outlined in Matthew 6:6–13 so that we might use them more effectively. Christ intended for us to pray with power. He above anyone else recognized that throughout our lives as Christians we would be involved in a constant struggle against the

STEP 1: Unclouding the Issue.

STEP 2: Unveiling before God.

STEP 8: Unleashing the Power of God.

STEP 3: Unconditional Surrender.

"PRAYER DIAMOND"

STEP 7: Uncovering His Truth.

STEP 4: Understanding the Source.

STEP 6: Uncovering the Negative Trends of my Life.

STEP 5: Understanding the Needs and "Debts" of my Life.

forces of evil in this world. Sometimes the evil is simply the character traits, habits, and personality patterns which lie deep within our own selves. Other times the evil we combat is viciously evident in the society around us, requiring us to be spiritually well-equipped, vigilant, and persistent in our Christian walk. Whatever form of spiritual combat we find ourselves engaged in, however, we must be able to pray readily and with power in order to be successful. The principles of the Lord's Prayer in Matthew 6:6–13 are inerrant and eternal. The goal of this simple tool, the "Prayer Diamond," is to enable you better to impliment these principles of powerful praying in your life.

Study Questions

1. What is the real common denominator in every study of prayer?
2. In your own words what is prayer?
3. How do we become transparent before God?
4. What in your words is the purpose of prayer?
5. What four things should we allow our mind to meditate on in the beginning of our prayer time?
6. 1 Corinthians 9:19–20 gives the reason we should completely commit our all to God. What does it say?

The Spiritual Gift God Has Given You

The king's daughter is all glorious within: her clothing is of wrought gold (Ps. 45:13).

As daughters of the King we must "dress" our spirit in such a way as to destroy wrong attitudes, negative thinking, guilt, self-hatred, and hurtful memories. The key to a smooth look in your clothes is the right undergarment. The key to healthy emotions which cause your life to run more smoothly is the undergarment of self-acceptance. Such self-acceptance begins in the spirit. (See Self-Acceptance Quiz on p. 223.)

We must accept our abilities. When Moses complained about his lack of ability when it came to doing the job God asked him to do, God asked a strange question: "Moses, what's that in your hand?" Moses just held up the old rough stick he had used to walk with. When that stick was yielded to the Lord it was used to part the

Red Sea, get water out of rocks, and became the handiest tool
Moses ever dreamed of. God doesn't demand that we create our
own abilities, He just asks us to use what we have. Use it and don't
ever feel inferior to another.

Natural abilities are not necessarily what our spiritual gift will
be. While I have some creative abilities that I was born with that
need to be brought under the control of the Holy Spirit, I also have
a spiritual gift that, when properly used, plays an important part in
the body of Christ. Now, whether I am a foot or an eye is not
important. Each gift is as important as the other.

There has been much interest over the recent years in the proper
discovery and understanding of spiritual gifts. In Romans 12:3–9
the seven intrinsic or "motivational" gifts of the Holy Spirit are
listed. They are:

1. Prophecy–the declaring of biblical truth.
2. Serving–the meeting of practical needs in the body of
   Christ.
3. Teaching–the research and examination of scriptural truths
   for sharing with other believers.
4. Exhorting–the encouraging and personal equipping of other
   Christians.
5. Giving–the meeting of primarily financial needs through
   contributions of all kinds.
6. Administration or ruling–the organizing of the body of
   Christ for the purpose of accomplishing tasks.
7. Mercy–empathizing with and emotionally uplifting fellow
   Christians.

The following is a spiritual gifts inventory composed of seventy
questions which should take approximately 25–30 minutes to
complete. We would like to thank Rob Guenther of Edmonton,
Alberta, Canada for his gracious assistance in developing this spiritual gifts inventory.

The G/B Spiritual Gifts Inventory

Instructions: For each statement, decide if that statement is MORE likely or LESS likely to describe you. There are no right or wrong answers here, only preferences. Respond by placing an "M" for MORE likely or an "L" for LESS likely in the blank next to each statement. The small letters to the left of each set of blanks will be used in scoring the inventory and should be covered up by a ruler or a folded piece of paper while you are completing the inventory.

"M" "L"

(a) ____ ____ 1. I am able to recognize what responsibilities can or cannot be delegated.

(p) ____ ____ 2. Discerning the character and motives of people is easy for me.

(g) ____ ____ 3. I absolutely enjoy seeing a gift of mine being an answer to someone's specific prayer.

(m) ____ ____ 4. I feel especially comfortable when I'm around individuals who are very sensitive to the feelings of others.

(e) ____ ____ 5. I like to associate and make plans with "action-oriented" people.

(p) ____ ____ 6. Speaking or declaring my position on matters is always important to me.

(g) ____ ____ 7. I'm good at handling money and making wise investments.

(p) ____ ____ 8. My commitment to the sovereignty of God is quite possibly my strongest tool for influencing other Christians.

(m) ____ ____ 9. The emotional atmosphere with an individual or in a group is something I readily and easily sense.

(t) ____ ____ 10. I see truth from the Bible as something you really have to dig for if you want quality.

"M" "L"

(g) ___ ___ 11. I almost always seek counsel before making a special financial gift above my routine tithe.

(s) ___ ___ 12. Remembering the specific likes and dislikes of people comes easy for me.

(p) ___ ___ 13. When I speak in public I am often frank and direct; sometimes my speech is seen as being harsh.

(g) ___ ___ 14. My giving is frequently a tool I use specifically to motivate others to financially support the Lord's work.

(t) ___ ___ 15. To be honest, I enjoy doing the research behind a lesson I may prepare more than the actual presenting of it.

(p) ___ ___ 16. When I see others violate the truth of Scripture, it causes me personally the most intense form of inner pain.

(a) ___ ___ 17. I like to get things done as fast as possible, and sometimes I'll sacrifice neatness for speed.

(g) ___ ___ 18. I enjoy finding a need and meeting it without anyone even knowing I was responsible.

(e) ___ ___ 19. I have a hard time staying interested in even a beautiful church service if I can't find several practical applications.

(a) ___ ___ 20. When a job is done, my first thought is to look for a new challenge to get involved with and keep myself busy.

(t) ___ ___ 21. When I hear a significant new idea, I often remember it or write it down and compare it later with other truths I know from Scripture.

(s) ___ ___ 22. Although like everyone else I thrive on sincere appreciation for my work, I seem to be

"M" "L"

able more than most to detect insincerity in
the praise of others.

(m) ____ ____ 23. When I am told of a difficult situation, my
first impulse is to remove hurt and bring
emotional healing to the people involved.

(g) ____ ____ 24. When I see a need to be met in others, I
may wait on meeting that need simply in
order to be able to give a more high quality
gift.

(a) ____ ____ 25. Seeing all the pieces of a project come together and work smoothly is a source of
great fulfillment to me. I like to be a project
coordinator.

(p) ____ ____ 26. A person may claim inward conviction, but
I will often demand outward evidences of
change before I will embrace that someone
in fellowship.

(m) ____ ____ 27. In a group setting, I seem to be the one who
feels the most responsible that everyone
feels accepted.

(p) ____ ____ 28. I insist on validating my decisions, often
even small ones, by direct scriptural pas-
sages.

(a) ____ ____ 29. People seek my counsel when they need an
overall practical picture of a situation, especially when long-term goals need to be
clarified.

(s) ____ ____ 30. I find much more enjoyment in reaching
short-term goals than in attempting to reach
long-range ones.

(e) ____ ____ 31. Finding concepts in the Scriptures which parallel everyday human experiences is some-
thing I enjoy doing and it seems to come
relatively easy to me.

(s) ____ ____ 32. When a project I am working on gets stalled,

"M" "L"

I feel I should use my personal time, energy, and money if necessary to assure that it stays on schedule.

(a) ___ ___ 33. I am not excessively bothered by negative criticism from co-workers if it is required in order to accomplish the ultimate task.

(p) ___ ___ 34. I am interested to have others point out my blind spots, especially in areas of biblical truth.

(t) ___ ___ 35. I cringe with disapproval when I hear a biblical illustration not used exactly in its proper doctrinal context.

(t) ___ ___ 36. I would be quite willing to change church memberships in order to sit under the instruction of accurate doctrinal teaching, regardless of less "warmth" in the new fellowship.

(s) ___ ___ 37. I often wait to get involved in activities until I see a need that no one else is meeting, then I usually am strongly drawn to meet that need.

(g) ___ ___ 38. I tend to see needs that others have, especially financial or practical ones, which might go otherwise unnoticed by some church members.

(s) ___ ___ 39. I have a hard time saying no when asked to do things and therefore get involved in a large variety of activities.

(g) ___ ___ 40. Public acknowledgment of my giving makes me uncomfortable; I would rather give quietly to worthwhile projects.

(m) ___ ___ 41. People in distress seem drawn to me and sometimes readily share deeply personal aspects of their problems with me.

(g) ___ ___ 42. When I make a contribution to a ministry, I

"M" "L"

develop a feeling of strong responsibility to the Lord for the quality and integrity of that ministry, even if I am not personally involved in its day to day operation.

(e) ____ ____ 43. Teaching without practical steps to applications seems to upset me more than it does most of my friends.

(s) ____ ____ 44. When everyone is tired on a work project, I seem to be one of the most able to maintain the stamina necessary to keep working on the task; and I find myself often using my energy to meet the needs of my co-workers who are feeling worn out.

(s) ____ ____ 45. When I hear that a job is going to require extra work and long hours, it seems to make me want to get involved all the more.

(t) ____ ____ 46. I am one who places great emphasis on the accuracy of the words a person uses.

(m) ____ ____ 47. I have noticed that I often feel strained and uncomfortable around individuals who are not very sensitive to the needs of others.

(e) ____ ____ 48. I like to be involved in projects where specific goals are targeted for action and precise scriptural steps are given to fulfill those goals.

(a) ____ ____ 49. If there is no structured leadership in a situation, I am often the one who assumes responsibility to get things organized.

(t) ____ ____ 50. I enjoy the challenge of doing research to validate a biblical truth.

(e) ____ ____ 51. When I am speaking or sharing with others, I seem to be intensely aware of visible signs of acceptance or rejection of what I am communicating.

(s) ____ ____ 52. Although I may be patient in certain areas,

"M"   "L"

when it comes to meeting needs in other people, I become frustrated if I can't act quickly to meet those needs.

(t) ____ ____ 53. I think the most important function of the pastor is the systematic saturation of his congregation with detailed biblical truths from his personal research and study. (If it takes you more than 5 minutes to answer this question, mark it "M".)

(p) ____ ____ 54. When considering an action, my first thoughts are about what kind of impact it will have on God's reputation in the community and His holiness.

(m) ____ ____ 55. Being firm with someone is usually my last recourse when dealing with a touchy situation.

(a) ____ ____ 56. I seem to be able to lay my hands quickly on the resources necessary to accomplish even difficult tasks, and others have asked me to help organize projects in the past.

(s) ____ ____ 57. I relish getting involved in projects, especially when the objective is to meet a practical need.

(a) ____ ____ 58. I don't really feel comfortable beginning a day unless I've taken some time to organize the activities I need to accomplish. I usually try to keep a list of things I need to get done.

(m) ____ ____ 59. I am quite sensitive towards an action which will hurt the feelings of other people.

(a) ____ ____ 60. When facing a job, I am quite conscious of the amount of time I have to accomplish it, and I am frustrated when personal problems slow down efficiency.

(e) ____ ____ 61. In the midst of serious problems and trials

"M" "L"

in someone's life, it is relatively easy for me to see how such difficulties can produce a new level of Christian maturity in their life.

(p) ___ ___ 62. Identifying and defining sin with a strong ability to hate evil is one of my most pronounced qualities.

(t) ___ ___ 63. When exposed to new biblical truths, I feel obliged to challenge the knowledge of those teaching (not necessarily in a negative way, but just to be sure that their biblical background is sound).

(e) ___ ___ 64. I enjoy getting together with other Christians one-on-one or in small groups to work out new solutions to scriptural problems.

(m) ___ ___ 65. When I am around other Christians who are suffering, I quickly sense their mental distress and often suffer emotionally along with them.

(t) ___ ___ 66. I feel that a working understanding of the Greek and Hebrew languages in which the original Bible manuscripts were written is necessary for someone to be a Bible scholar.

(m) ___ ___ 67. Often I will avoid firmness in trying to spare the feelings of others, even if I appear weak or indecisive because of it.

(e) ___ ___ 68. I appear to disregard the feelings of those I'm counseling at times because I place such a high emphasis on taking steps of action to solve problems.

(g) ___ ___ 69. Knowing the worth of a project and understanding fully the intentions of its sponsors is my primary consideration when giving to a project.

(e) ___ ___ 70. When I use Scripture for practical applications, it may appear that I am taking it out of context to some extent.

Instructions for Scoring

Once you have completed the inventory, score each of the seven spiritual gifts as follows. For the spiritual gift of prophecy, go back over the test and count all of the questions with a small "p" to the left of them in which you placed an "M" as the answer. (You will not count any questions in which you placed an "L" in the answer blank.) Once you have counted all the questions marked by the small letter "p" to which you answered "M," place that number in the blank just to the left of the word *prophecy* on the Scoring Graph below. (The number should be somewhere between 0–10). Once you have placed the number in the blank to the left of the word *prophecy* indicating how many "M" answers you gave to questions marked by the small letter "p", then blacken in the corresponding number of squares in the row to the right of the word *prophecy*. Now score the remaining six gifts in the same way. Once you have done this for all seven of the spiritual gifts included in this inventory, you will have a bar graph indicating which motivational gifts are your most prominent.

SCORING GRAPH

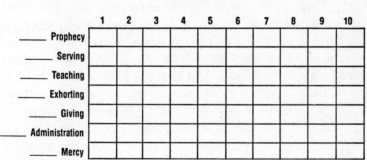

	1	2	3	4	5	6	7	8	9	10
_____ Prophecy										
_____ Serving										
_____ Teaching										
_____ Exhorting										
_____ Giving										
_____ Administration										
_____ Mercy										

Using Your Gift

Once you have determined which of the seven gifts of the spirit are your most prominent, then it is important that you realize that God would have you serve with that gift or gifts. If one of your gifts is prophecy, then you will tend to be persuasive in speech and you will enjoy bringing to light things that are not clear to other people. You will tend to gravitate toward that which is good and away from that which is evil, but you will have to be careful not to be critical. Love without hypocrisy is a major need of the person with the gift of prophecy. The importance which you have in the body of Christ is emphasized in 1 Corinthians 14:1 (NASB) which says, "Pursue love, yet desire earnestly spiritual gifts, but especially that you may prophesy." Your willingness to proclaim biblical truth openly is a key contribution to the members of the body of Christ.

If your most prominent gift is serving, then you will be especially able to discern the needs of people. You will probably be willing to endure personal discomfort and overlook your own requirements in the pursuit of meeting the needs of others. You must be responsible and not impulsive, and you must be willing to allow others to receive recognition, not hoping secretly to be singled out for special praise. You must be careful not to become proud of your works, and you must be especially sensitive not to prematurely meet the needs of others before they have a chance to realize those needs or before God has a chance to use those needs to build character into their lives. Individuals with the gift of serving have a tendency to become bitter over time when their hard work is not recognized or appreciated, and you must avoid this. The key verse for maintaining your perspective as a Christian with the gift of serving is Colossians 3:23–24 (NASB), "Whatever you do, do your work heartily, as for the Lord rather than for men; knowing that from the Lord you will receive the reward of the inheritance. It is the Lord Christ whom you serve."

If your gift is teaching then you will love to dig out the facts concerning the Scriptures and also to accumulate knowledge on the more exhausting details of the Bible. You must be careful while being diligent in the details of your work not to develop spiritual "tunnel vision." This "tunnel vision" means concentrating on the details of a particular fund of information rather than communicating the basic principles of Christian living. Christians with the spiritual gift of teaching have a tendency to become spiritually obese, being overbalanced in the accumulation of knowledge and underbalanced in the degree of application in their lives. Beware that you do not become more interested in finding truth than you are in ministering Christ's love to your fellow Christians. The importance of teaching the Word of God clearly and accurately is reflected by the Apostle Paul's instructions to his young disciple, Timothy, "Be diligent to present yourself approved to God as a workman who does not need to be ashamed, handling accurately the word of truth" (2 Tim. 2:15, NASB).

If the spiritual gift of exhortation is one with which God has blessed you, then you will be drawn into personal counseling of other Christians. You will find yourself rejoicing in one-on-one contacts which result in life-changing decisions. You must always rejoice in hope and be patient with others who are slow to progress. Persistent prayer may not be as exciting to you as the friction of direct exhortation, and yet it will probably be the consistency of your prayer life which determines the degree to which God will be able to bless your exhortation and encouragement in the lives of others. You must be careful not to boast in the personal results of your ministry and certainly you will have to learn to deal with discouragement due to failures in the lives of other people. Be careful not to motivate others through the use of short-term games such as meeting their more selfish needs, but be selective in sharing truth with those individuals who will cherish it and apply it over the long run. You will find yourself rallying to such verses as these: "And we proclaim Him, admonishing every man and teaching every man with all wisdom, that we may present every man complete in Christ. Encourage one another day after day, as long as it is still called "Today," lest any one of you be hardened by the deceitfulness of sin" (Col. 1:28, Heb. 3:13, NASB).

If you have been blessed with the spiritual gift of giving, you will find that you are motivated to divert your personal assets to meet the needs of and further the ministries of others. You will seem to have the ability to make sometimes immediate decisions which may "make the difference" in the times of crisis in another person's ministry. God will entrust you with the financial and physical resources to be empowered to help others when He taps you on the shoulder and shows you an opportunity. You must be aware that you do not become proud of the wealth of resources which God entrusts you, and you must be careful never to measure the success of other people by their material assets. You must be as willing to give genuinely to meet the needs of a stranger as you are to meet the needs of someone personally close to you. The gift of giving has been bestowed upon you not so that you can selectively shower your friends with assistance, but so that you can be a ready-made tool in the hand of God to meet the needs throughout the body of Christ. The joy and prosperity which God will extend to you as you properly utilize this gift are truly exciting, "Give, and it will be given to you; good measure, pressed down, shaken together, running over, they will pour into your lap. For whatever measure you deal out to others, it will be dealt to you in return" (Luke 6:38, NASB).

The gift of administration is crucial to the proper organization and maintenance of the New Testament Church. If this is your gift, you will notice that you seem to have the ability to coordinate activities within a group toward the accomplishment of a common goal. You will be gifted in the ability to distinguish major objectives from the less crucial ones around them. As others watch you in action, they will sense that you are an individual who can shrewdly accomplish a task efficiently. Of course, some will feel threatened by your ability to move decisively and with efficiency, and you must be willing to "bless those who curse you." Pride in one's power to excel is a real danger to the individual with the gift of administration. Also, you must be wary not to "use" people in order to accomplish goals, but rather be sure that you maintain Christ's perspective of having a ministry in the lives of people. A dangerous tendency in those individuals with the gift of administration is overlooking major character faults in those who are useful to reaching goals. Paul states in 1 Timothy 3:4 (NASB) that the ability to be adequate to the task of administration is important enough to require it of elders: "He must be one who manages his own household well."

If the spiritual gift God has blessed you with is mercy, then you will find yourself motivated to feel empathy with the misfortunes and miseries of others. You will be the first in the crowd on many occasions to mentally and emotionally relate to another person who is suffering. You will feel the need to help others feel accepted, and other people may tell you things which they have not entrusted to any other person. You will find that you are able to share the happiest of times with others and also enter into grief with those who are in deep sorrow. You must be careful not to resent those who seem insensitive to personal needs, and you must be careful not to let your logic be guided by your emotions. You will have a tendency to fail to be firm when it is necessary, and it will be difficult for you to enforce biblical priorities when you know that such actions may "hurt" someone else. As an individual with the gift of mercy, however, you will in many ways be able to reflect Christ's own attitude toward others. "And so, as those who have been chosen of God, holy and beloved, put on a heart of compassion, kindness, humility, gentleness and patience" (Col. 2:12, NASB).

Study Questions

1. Why do you think we must enjoy self-acceptance?
2. After taking the spiritual gift test, share with the group what gift is most prominent in your life.
3. What have you learned about using your gift?

Chapter 18
Restoring the Spirit

What Spiritual "Type" Are You?

Through the previous chapters as we have looked at many aspects of human behavior, we have seen just how complex an organism we humans are. We have looked at the mechanisms by which we can effectively cleanse, exercise, feed, clothe, and restore both the body and soul. We've also examined the spirit and have come to appreciate that in the proper care of the spirit lies the secret to true fulfillment in life. In restoring the spirit, it is useful to see that God has given us an example of the two spiritual "types" of women. As we examine the behavior of two women whom Christ loved very much, Mary and Martha, we begin to see a pattern emerging which has tremendous significance for today's woman as she seeks spiritual renewal and restoration. A clear understanding of the spiritual attributes and actions of Mary and Martha will point the way toward renewing each woman's own spiritual vigor. There are two major passages of Scripture in which Mary and Martha are compared. One involves a situation of *suffering* (John

11:18–25) and the other involves a situation of *service* (Luke 10:38–42).

A *Situation of Suffering* (John 11:18–25)

In John 11 we find the story of the resurrection of Lazarus from the dead. Mary, Martha, and their brother Lazarus were three of Christ's closest personal friends. It is obvious that He spent much time with them, and although they were not members of the twelve disciples, they were a significant source of encouragement and support to Him during His ministry. When Lazarus became ill and died, Jesus was away ministering in another place. After he was told of Lazarus' death, he returned to the home of Mary, Martha, and Lazarus in Bethany. When he arrived on the scene, Lazarus had already been dead for four days. The grief, confusion, and despair were overwhelming. Mary, Martha, and the little Christian community of which they were a part stood in shock. In this apparently tragic situation, we are exposed to the two very different spiritual responses of Mary and Martha. Notice the comparison below from John 11:18–45.

MARY'S BEHAVIOR	MARTHA'S BEHAVIOR
1. She awaited to be called and consoled (v. 20, 28).	1. She initiated confrontation (v. 20).
2. She was desperate, and ran to Him (falling at His feet). She was emotionally hungry inside (v. 29, 32a).	2. She was disappointed and rebuked Him (demanding an explanation). She was emotionally angry inside (v. 21).
3. She didn't have a doctrinal statement to share, but through faith she *responded* to His Person (v. 32b), assuming that	3. She was able to state a biblical principle in the midst of a distressing situation, but through doubt she rationalized away His

His very presence would somehow bring sufficiency for the situation.

4. She wept with great emotion over the pain of the situation, then followed Christ to the tomb (without Him ever telling her that He intended to raise her brother Lazarus from the dead). In other words, she went from the emotional (experiential) to the analytical (factual) in her reasoning (v. 33–34). She was emotionally expressive.

5. She simply confessed her need of the Lord and saw the *fruit* of His plan (v. 45).

power, minimizing the possibility that Jesus could literally change the course of human events through a miracle (v. 22–24).

4. She used her analytical understanding of who Christ was to help her believe what He could do. In other words, she went from the analytical (factual) to the emotional (experiential) in her reasoning (v. 27). She was emotionally reserved.

5. She second-guessed the Lord and saw the *flaws* of His plan (vs. 39).

We can see the different spiritual orientations of Mary and Martha by contrasting their responses to this situation of intense suffering surrounding the death of their brother Lazarus. Another passage of Scripture in which we see them clearly contrasted is Luke 10:38–42. Here they are not involved in a situation of suffering but rather a situation in which they are relating to Christ, listening to Him converse, and meeting some of His personal needs.

A *Situation of Service* (Luke 10:38–42)

MARY'S BEHAVIOR   MARTHA'S BEHAVIOR

1. She saw a relationship and moved to enjoy it (v. 39).

1. She saw a need, and moved to meet it (v. 38).

2. She was *well-pleased,* enthralled with the person of Jesus (vs. 39–41).

2. She was *well-organized,* involved in the preparation of dinner (v. 40).

3. She concentrated on the presence of Jesus as her primary activity (v. 39–41).

3. She complained about the lack of interest Jesus showed in her activities (v. 40).

4. She was *people*-oriented (v. 30–41).

4. She was *projects*-oriented (v. 41).

5. The attributes of a relationship encouraged her and a shortage of time prompted her to be more and more interested in relating to Christ (v. 39–41).

5. The arrangement of things concerned her greatly and a shortage of time prompted her to be more and more distracted with busy work (v. 41).

6. Her moments were taken up making investments in people, which last for eternity (v. 42).

6. Her moments were taken up making investments in projects, which last only for a season (v. 42).

In these situations of suffering and service, we see two very different ways of relating to Jesus from Mary and Martha. Many, many women who are tirelessly laboring within the church are spiritually modeling Martha. They are compelled by an inner drive to meet the needs of others, sometimes at the expense of developing a personal relationship with Jesus Christ. Because their contributions to their local churches are so strategically important, their malnourishment in a real spiritual relationship with Jesus can go unnoticed. They are so available, helpful, and tirelessly longsuffering in the discharge of their many church-related responsibilities that no one even thinks to wonder whether they are spiritually "dying on the vine." A large proportion of my counseling is with these "Marthas" of the modern church. That is not to say that women who are spiritually more similar to Mary don't have problems as well, but the classical "workaholic" Christian Martha is a setup for a spiritual burnout in the latter half of her life. She starts the race well with intense enthusiasm and vigor, but she may finish poorly because of chronic spiritual malnourishment and overwork in meeting the seemingly endless needs of others.

In the two sections that follow, we will examine some of the traits, actions, and emotional patterns which characterize the Marys and Marthas of the modern church.

Potentially Positive and Negative Characteristics of a Woman with *Mary's* Personality Pattern

1. She has a good personality, is likeable, and is outgoing.
2. She is fun to be with, "the life of the party."
3. She is emotional and easily excited.
4. She emphasizes feelings and lives in the present.
5. She is vain about her personal physical appearance.
6. She is dependent, at times even gullible.
7. She relies much more on feelings than she does on thinking, and sometimes her logic is poor.
8. When under stress she may cope with life by using denial (hoping and believing problems will just go away by themselves).
9. She is very open and warm, sharing much about herself very quickly.
10. She can be charming, vivacious, and gracious.
11. In her weaker moments she is immature and manipulative.
12. In men she often looks for a father figure, someone upon whom she can depend.
13. Her behavior may appear to be attention-seeking and her language is often filled with dramatic statements.
14. She overreacts easily in emotional situations.
15. She is generous, sensitive, and sometimes extravagant in her desire to encourage others.
16. She is suggestible and may be easily taken advantage of.
17. She is impulsive, at times undisciplined.
18. Everyday, unexciting tasks are tiresome or burdensome to her; she does not like routine work.
19. Detailed planning frustrates her.

20. Being on time is not one of her strong points.
21. She often appears to be disorganized.
22. She is sensitive and quite verbally expressive.
23. She exaggerates when dramatizing a point and listeners find themselves enthralled by her speech and mannerisms.
24. She has a good imagination and a rich fantasy life.
25. She sometimes feels threatened by the competition of other physically attractive or seductive females.
26. At her worst she seeks to manipulate members of the opposite sex through seduction.
27. She can be a hypochondriac and others often feel that her physical problems have an emotional cause.
28. Her daydreams and fantasies tend to center around receiving love and attention.
29. Often she had a childhood in which she had some special position in the family, such as being the only female or the "baby" of the family.
30. Her mother may have been cold or jealous toward her normally, yet her mother tended to be warm and very supportive when she was sick.
31. She may have had and may still have a relationship of dependence with her mother that keeps her from fully growing up.
32. She probably had a very long tomboy stage as a teenager and may still enjoy direct competition with men.
33. She was probably very close to her father in the first six years of her life; and other family members may describe her as having been "Daddy's favorite."
34. While growing up, her father encouraged her to be emotionally expressive (he may have done this directly by verbal statements, or indirectly by reinforcing certain behaviors).
35. In the teenage years, her girl friends were often less attractive than she.
36. She tends to experience obvious mood changes.
37. Seeing the opposite sex realistically is difficult for her; she tends to idealize certain men.

38. In an environment where there are several attractive men, she will be prone to compete for their attention.
39. She has spiritual ups and downs, and when things are down she tends to blame the devil for everything going wrong.
40. She is very excitable in her religious experiences, and may even claim certain special gifts, powers, or visitations from the Lord.
41. She is frequently angry at God when things don't go her way or when things occur that she doesn't understand.
42. Her sinful temptations tend to be predominately in the sexual area or in the area of bitterness toward dominant, overbearing, competitive females.

Potentially Positive and Negative Characteristics of a Woman with *Martha's* Personality Pattern

1. She is neat, clean, and orderly.
2. She is perfectionistic, meticulous, and conscientious.
3. She may work too hard and be unable to relax.
4. Her conscience is very strict, and sometimes she is rigid and inflexible with other people.
5. She has a history of being a very good student, and seems to achieve well in academic settings.
6. With others she prefers to stay on the level of theories and ideas rather than sharing feelings and personal needs.
7. She may keep her emotions a secret from others and tend to "feel" with her mind. Others may say she is too logical.
8. She is visibly competitive, and below the surface has a tremendous need to maintain control and power in situations.
9. Ironically, she may display some opposite traits, for example, being orderly in most areas of her life but very untidy in a handful of others or being very responsible in major tasks assigned to her, yet uncharacteristically negligent in a small number of others.
10. At times she feels very drawn between obedience and defiance, but obedience usually wins.

11. She is anti-authority on occasion. Usually when she resists authority it is by subtly indirect means rather than blatantly direct ones.
12. Others see her as being a very stable and steady person at all times.
13. She may seem interpersonally cold or aloof due to her interest in facts and not feelings.
14. She is afraid of feelings of warmth found in intensely personal one-to-one relationships. Such relationships may make her uncomfortable or nervous.
15. She often lives in the future, postponing pleasure and relaxation for herself. She often feels guilty when she is enjoying herself "too much."
16. She lacks enthusiasm and spontaneity.
17. She continually needs respect and security, and is usually a very moral person.
18. She fears the loss of control in a situation, especially in interpersonal relationships, and thus may be reluctant to commit herself to close relationships with others.
19. She tends to focus on irrelevant details, being insecure when things are not well-planned.
20. She has hidden inside her feelings of powerlessness and a sense of futility to control the outcome of her own life.
21. She is extremely self-willed, even obstinately stubborn at times.
22. Words and intellectual rationalizations are used by her to put off and avoid dealing with unpleasant situations.
23. She has a need to appear correct, perfect, and in control at all times.
24. She is really only comfortable when she knows all the facts about a situation she is dealing with, and she never feels that she has prepared quite enough for any test, speaking engagement, or activity that she is about to engage in.
25. She is reliable and dependable in nearly everything she does.
26. She is persistent and will work at something for a long time to accomplish her goal.

27. She is disciplined, and she likes lists and schedules.
28. She is frugal and watches her money closely.
29. She is punctual, priding herself on being on time and having little patience with others who are chronically late.
30. She is very good at tasks that require intense concentration.
31. Her parents were not usually the type that were emotional in showing love, and she may have felt accepted on a conditional performance basis.
32. In her thinking, most things are black or white.
33. She becomes quite impatient with herself when she is having trouble making a decision.
34. She tends to be critical of others and has a precise eye for flaws.
35. She dislikes change, especially unannounced change.
36. Submission within the marriage commitment is difficult; she prefers co-existence where each partner in the marriage is allowed to pursue his or her own interests.
37. She may save for a tomorrow that never arrives, putting off self-indulgence for "another day."
38. She has trouble admitting mistakes, and can't stand criticism.
39. In marriage, she tends to do most of the thinking for her mate.
40. Sex to her is unspontaneous, routine, and often without much intimacy.
41. Theologically, she insists on precision even in minor doctrinal issues, and may doubt her own salvation because she sees herself as not having been "worthy" enough to be saved.
42. She tends to be a chronic worrier.

There are positive and negative spiritual traits in both Mary's and Martha's lists above. The important issue here is that, as a woman of God, you find many of your more positive and negative spiritual characteristics in the lists above. Having found those characteristics, develop a plan to accept yourself with both the good and bad qualities you have noted. God is completely aware of every minute thought and characteristic. He may not *approve* of everything you do, think, or feel, but He *accepts* you unconditionally at all times. Acceptance does not depend upon approval. The first key to maximizing your strengths and minimizing your weaknesses is learning to accept yourself as having been made in the image of God. This begins with a transparent acknowledgment of the totality of your being before the Lord. Self-acceptance is the indispensable first step on the path out of the dark tunnel of personal spiritual despair. If you can begin to accept yourself completely, then God can begin to empower you to change those things about yourself which you accept but do not particularly approve of.

The following is a simple quiz composed of twelve questions to be answered either yes or no. The quiz is designed to help you determine whether you really accept yourself.

Self-Acceptance Quiz

Yes/No

_____ 1. Do you lose patience quickly with others when they don't get things done up to your standards?

_____ 2. Do you question whether you are really loved by God?

_____ 3. Is it very important to you that other people know when you were in the "right" in a situation in which there was a disagreement?

_____ 4. Are you easily tempted to judge others by their exterior: their looks, their background, their job, etc.?

_____ 5. Are you very sensitive about your own appearance, the appearance of your children, or the appearance of your spouse?

_____ 6. Do you take on too many responsibilities, trying to please nearly every one?

_____ 7. Do you find yourself getting jealous or envious easily?
_____ 8. Do you tend to put yourself down in front of other people?
_____ 9. Are you easily hurt or disappointed by people?
_____ 10. Do you secretly yearn for the compliments of others when you've completed a task?
_____ 11. Does constructive criticism from others really "get you down"?
_____ 12. Do you ever daydream about being someone else, or about having led a completely different life?

If you answered yes to several of these questions, then it may well be that you are struggling with self-acceptance. If self-acceptance is not readily available to a woman, then a daily sense of security, well-being, and belief in herself is very difficult to maintain. God is not pleased when we artificially concoct a false sense of pride or self-confidence based on our own abilities apart from Him. Yet, it has been said that God cannot use a discouraged Christian, and lack of self-acceptance lies at the very heart of discouragement. When we accept ourselves, then we also are accepting what God can do through us. Then 1 John 4:4 (NASB) can became a reality in our lives. "You are from God, little children, and have overcome them; because greater is He that is in you than he who is in the world."

If self-acceptance is such a crucial ingredient to spiritual good health, then we need to examine some steps to self-acceptance.

Four Steps to Spiritual Self-Acceptance

Step 1: *Concentrate (or meditate) on the truth.* The truest thing about yourself is what God says about you in His Word. Romans 12:2 says that we are to be transformed by the renewing of our mind. The promise is that when our minds are renewed, we will be transformed. This transformation will render us able to prove (attain) in our daily living God's choicest will for our lives. Not only do we want to *know* God's will, but we also want to *live* it. God says that you must believe in your innermost spirit that He is for you not against you. He accepts you not on the basis of what you do, but on the basis of what He did for you in Christ Jesus. Once we have accepted Jesus Christ as our personal Savior, then it's as if God puts on a special pair of glasses for viewing our lives. These glasses are shaded with the sacrificial blood of Jesus Christ, and when we are viewed by God through these glasses, He sees only the sufficiency of Christ in our lives, not the woeful inadequacy of our own abilities. By the firm intention of your will, you must decide that this is so. The Scriptures say that,

> For by grace are ye saved through faith; that not of yourselves: it is the gift of God: not of works, lest any man should boast. For we are his workmanship, created in Christ Jesus unto good works, which God hath before ordained that we should walk in them (Eph. 2:8–10).

We have an inner willingness or unwillingness to focus upon the worthiness which was assigned to us by God through the work of Christ. He has chosen us to be His ambassadors, and it is our understanding and application of this truth that determines what we will become. If we meditate on what we've achieved or failed to achieve, what we're ashamed of, or even on what we've wished for in our lives, then we are destined to be discouraged. Seeking or imagining for ourselves a lifestyle that's anything other than a headlong pursuit of His person will inevitably lead to a lack of self-acceptance. We can never be all we can be until we allow Christ to be all He wishes to be within us. Giving Him free rein in our lives involves claiming by faith that we are not only His children, but worthy instruments in this world.

Step 2: *Dwell on the positive.* Determine that you are going to search relentlessly for the positive potential in any situation. Dr. Robert Schuller has called this, "Changing your scars into stars." There are positive potentials in every situation, regardless of how utterly dismal the circumstances may seem. An often misunderstood passage of Scripture which deals with this matter of understanding difficult circumstances is Romans 8:28–29:

> And we know that God causes all things to work together for good to those who love God, to those who are called according to His purpose. For whom He foreknew, He also predestined to be conformed to the image of His Son, that He might be the first-born among many brethren.

This Scripture is teaching two very important points. First, that God has predestined us as Christians to be conformed to the image of His Son. In other words, He has a pattern specifically cut for each of us which (if we will allow that pattern to work itself out within our lives) will bring our character into conformity with the actual character of Jesus Christ. This is not some "pie in the sky" idea with no practical implications. It is a spiritual center-mast to which the godly woman must bind herself during the frightful tempests of tragedy which may blow through her life. If the Christian woman cannot hold fast to the belief that *every* event, both the joyful and the tragic, can be utilized to bring her further into conformity with Jesus Christ, then she will totally despair of the Christian faith.

The second major principle in Romans 8:28–29 is that all things can work together toward a good result, even without these things being good in themselves. Although the event itself may be completely terrible, the result can be wonderously positive. Unfortunately, some Christians would promote a form of "total bliss" theology in which the Christian simply perceives that nothing negative ever befalls him or her. All sickness can be cured, all debts can be absolved, all losses can be forgotten. This is simply not true and certainly not scriptural. Terrible events should hurt us terribly. A stone does not weep, and a tree does not have regrets, but we as human beings have been endowed with a full range of emotional and spiritual responses within our personality. To deny the reality of the impact of the trials of this life is to pretend that we're not real people; to ignore God's potential use of a situation for a positive result in our lives is to deny his sovereignty. The biblical patriarch Joseph captured the essence of Romans 8:28–29 when he described God's miraculously positive use of a terrible situation in his life:

And as for you, you meant evil against me, but God meant it for good in order to bring about this present result, to preserve many people alive (Gen. 50:20, NASB).

After having been nearly killed by his own family, sold into slavery, imprisoned, abused, and accused wrongfully, Joseph was able to realize that in spite of the tragedy of these events, God had brought about a positive result in the lives of many people. Many a person has been saved by a gospel message preached around the gravesite of a young child, and whole Christian communities have been challenged to revival by the testimony of a godly person going through the trials of a dread disease. It is foolish to try to minimize the impact of a tragedy on our lives, but it is even more foolish to refuse to see God giving us an opportunity for something positive to come out of it.

Step 3: *Thank God for everything.* We have just talked about dwelling on the positive potentials of any event occurring in our lives, regardless how tragic that event may be. In order to do this, we must allow our mind to dwell on things for which we can thank God. It has been said that the two attitudes of thankfulness and bitterness cannot coexist simultaneously in the same person. Attitudes of true thankfulness to God can build within us self-acceptance and confidence, replacing bitterness and doubt. In Colossians 3:1–2 we are told to keep seeking those things which are above where Christ is at work in our lives, and to set our minds on these things above, not on the things that are currently discouraging us.

Paul explains to us how we can maintain an attitude of thanksgiving to God in everything. He is giving us one of the keys to self-acceptance—believing that God intends to do us no harm and in fact that He strives against the forces of evil to provide for our best. Sometimes events may confound and overwhelm us, but we *must* maintain an attitude of thanksgiving to God. 1 Thessalonians 5:18 (NASB) states, "In everything give thanks; for this is God's will for you in Christ Jesus."

Things to Thank God For:
• Thank Him that Christ died for you.

- Thank Him that Christ is at work in your life in a loving way.
- Thank Him for specific things you like about yourself.
- Thank Him for specific things you haven't liked about yourself.
- Thank Him for the things He has given you in your life that you have enjoyed and cherished.
- Thank Him for the losses that you have undergone and the strength that He has supplied to see you through those losses.

Step 4: *Let God change you.* The Scriptures teach us that we are complete in Christ (Col. 2:10). Yet, it is by walking with Him in faith through a lifetime that we realize the fullness of this experience. We must daily draw upon His power to not only examine every area of our life, but also to acquire the ability to change progressively into His likeness. Unfortunately, many Christians insist on desperately clutching to the past, as if change represents a threat to them. It has been said that no one remains stationary in the Christian life; we either move ahead or drift backward. The Scriptures teach us in Galatians 2:20 that because we have been crucified with Christ, we now have Him living in us. And He lives in us to accomplish the specific purpose of progressively changing us into more righteous children of God. If we do not allow the Lord to change us into more mature Christians, then, the world will change us into less mature ones. We will either be shaped by the Holy Spirit into more Christlike Christians, or shaped by the world into more carnal ones. The choice is ours, and Christ explained the options which we have in Matthew 9:16–17. If we are willing to change into the newness of Christ, then we will experience the continual refreshing of a life controlled by Him. If we are unwilling to accept change and instead try to maintain the status quo, then we will find ourselves discouraged and stagnant in the outcome of our Christian life. Philippians 2:12–13 (NASB) teaches: "Work out your salvation with fear and trembling; for it is God who is at work in you, both to will and to work for His good pleasure." God would seek to change us, but we must be willing to accept the internal work of His Holy Spirit as it builds the principles of Scripture into our lives. Let us never be found futilely holding on to *sameness*, rather than real *saneness*. The choice is ours: either let God change us for the better, or circumstances will change us for the worse.

As you seek to direct your life into a healthy relationship with God, you may want to examine yourself by using the "Spiritual Health Checklist." This checklist is certainly not comprehensive, but it offers seven helpful guidelines by which we can evaluate the effectiveness of our spiritual life. As we seek to carry out our commitment to the Lord, personally knowing Him becomes the driving force of our lives. "Whom have I in heaven but Thee? And besides Thee (oh Lord), I desire nothing on earth. My flesh and my heart may fail; but God is the strength of our heart and my portion forever (Ps. 73:25–26, NASB).

Spiritual Health Checklist

Can I:

1. Express love openly? (John 13:35).
2. Deal constructively with reality, knowing it is God Who watches me continually and delivers me from the situations into which I fall? (Ps. 44:6–8; Isa. 66:2).
3. Redirect hostile impulses into active and constructive outlets? (Matt. 5:38–44).
4. Feel and express emotions appropriately? (John 11:33–35; Heb. 4:15).
5. Experience satisfaction from giving? (Luke 6:38; Mark 4:24).
6. Adapt to change? (Phil. 1:6; Matt. 9:16–17).
7. Relate satisfactorily with others? (Phil. 2:2–5).

As we seek to develop into all we can be within Christ Jesus, no one is more interested in the success of this process than God Himself. He literally wraps us in His arms and cares for us as a mother hen does her chicks. In Psalm 31:24 He tells us to be strong and take courage because we can hope in Him. In Isaiah 65:24 He says that He hears and begins to answer our prayers while we are still speaking them. In Joel 2:32 He promises that whosoever calls upon His name will be delivered. And finally, in Isaiah 53:12 He states that it was His own Son Who personally bore our sins and loved us enough to lay down His life, giving us abundant life now and eternal life in the future.

In this book we have attempted to focus on the three major functional areas of the human being: the body, the soul, and the spirit. Within each of these areas, our intent has been to examine its workings, its potentials, and its pitfalls. In doing so, it is our hope and prayer that we may have contributed in some small way to God's fulfilling His ultimate purpose in your life. The road to Christian maturity is certainly not always smooth. The emotional sandstorms, doctrinal quicksand, and situational avalanches can at times seem almost more than we can overcome. Yet, God has given us the promise of His Word against all such hindrances:

> What shall we then say to these things, if
> God be for us, who can be against us? (Rom. 8:31).

Study Questions

1. Would you consider yourself a Mary or a Martha?
2. Discuss the possibility of being so busy "serving" the Lord that we neglect developing a personal relationship with Him.
3. Did you take the self-acceptance quiz?
4. Discuss the four steps to spiritual self-acceptance.
5. Add to the list of things you can thank God for.
6. What does Matthew 9:16–17 teach us about being willing to change?
7. Has this book helped you better grasp the need for a balanced life? Will it work?